YORK NOTES

ENGLISH LANGUAGE
PRACTICE TESTS
WITH ANSWERS

Suitable for AQA, Edexcel, Eduqas and OCR

SUSANNAH WHITE

PEARSON

YORK PRESS

The right of Susannah White to be identified as the Author of this Work
has been asserted by her in accordance with the Copyright,
Designs and Patents Act 1988

YORK PRESS
322 Old Brompton Road, London SW5 9JH

PEARSON EDUCATION LIMITED
Edinburgh Gate, Harlow,
Essex CM20 2JE, United Kingdom
Associated companies, branches and representatives throughout the world

First published 2017

10 9 8 7 6 5 4 3 2 1

ISBN 978–1–2921–8632–0

Phototypeset by DTP Media
Printed in Slovakia

Photo credits: Syda Productions/Shutterstock for page 6 bottom / RTimages/Shutterstock
for page 22 top / David Vogt/Shutterstock for page 59 middle / Ana Blazic Pavlovic/
Shutterstock for page 64 top.

CONTENTS

PART ONE: INTRODUCTION

How to use these papers

This book contains four York Notes example GCSE English Language practice test papers: there are two Paper 1s (imaginative/creative texts) and two Paper 2s (non-fiction texts). All these York Notes papers have been modelled on the ones that you will sit in your GCSE 9–1 English Language exams, whether you are studying AQA, Edexcel, Eduqas or OCR.*

There are lots of ways these papers can support your study and revision for the GCSE 9–1 English Language exam. There is no 'right' way – choose the one or ones that suits your learning style best.

You could use them:

1 Alongside York Notes *English Language and Literature: Revision and Exam Practice*

Do you have the York Notes *Revision and Exam Practice* guide for GCSE English Language (and Literature)?

The papers in this book will allow you to try out the skills and techniques outlined in Chapters 1 to 6 of the guide. So you could:

● read a section of the guide dealing with one specific question type
● complete this question in one of the practice papers printed here.

2 As a stand-alone revision programme

Have you already mastered all of the skills needed for your exam?

Then you can keep your skills fresh by answering one or two questions from this book each day or week.

You could make a revision diary and allocate particular questions to particular times.

3 As a form of mock exam

Would you like to work under exam conditions?

You could put aside part of a day to work on a full paper in a quiet room. Set a stopwatch so that you can experience what it will be like in your real exam. If some of your friends have copies of this book then several of you could all do this together and discuss your answers afterwards.

4 As a combination of revision and exam practice

Would you like to do some revision and then try a mock exam?

Perhaps you could work through one set of papers slowly – question by question over a number of days – and then save the other set of papers to use as a mock nearer the exam.

*The paper numbers and content broadly match those of AQA, Edexcel and Eduqas. OCR reverses the order of the components.

How to use the answer sections

This book contains answer sections that will help you to understand what the examiners are looking for, and how your own responses compare against sample answers at a range of levels.

Sample answers show the key points and ideas you could have included.

The marking criteria tell you what the examiners are looking for.

Sample responses at different levels show you the difference between Higher, Mid and Lower Level work.

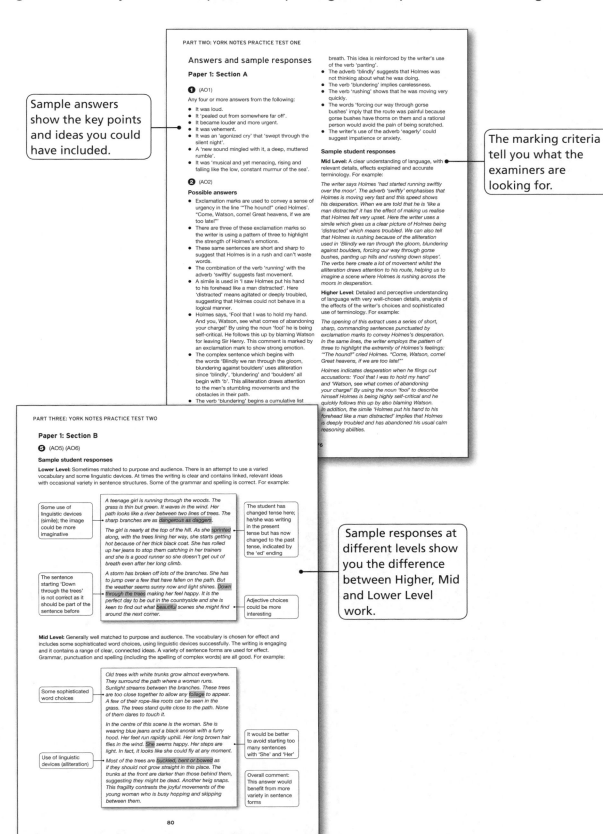

Assessment Objectives

Your work will be examined through the six Assessment Objectives (AOs) listed below. Each question in the practice papers is assessed by one or occasionally two of these.

Section A: Reading – Assessment Objectives

AO1	● Identify and interpret explicit and implicit information and ideas. ● Select and synthesise evidence from different texts.
AO2	● Explain, comment on and analyse how writers use language and structure to achieve effects and influence readers, using relevant subject terminology to support their views.
AO3	● Compare writers' ideas and perspectives, as well as how these are conveyed, across two or more texts.
AO4	● Evaluate texts critically and support this with appropriate textual references.

Section B: Writing – Assessment Objectives

AO5	● Communicate clearly, effectively and imaginatively, selecting and adapting tone, style and register for different forms, purposes and audiences. ● Organise information and ideas, using structural and grammatical features to support coherence and cohesion of texts.
AO6	● Use a range of vocabulary and sentence structures for clarity, purpose and effect, with accurate spelling and punctuation (20% of total marks).

AO coverage across the papers

The grids below show you the Assessment Objectives examined on each practice paper. As you can see, some AOs apply to both papers while others apply to only one paper. When it comes to preparing for your actual exam, make sure that you have checked the AO coverage across your own papers, as these vary across the different exam boards/organisations.

Remember to notice the number of marks allowed for each question as this will help you to gauge how much you should write and how much time you should spend on each question.

York Notes Practice Tests One and Two – Paper 1

Section	Question number	AO	Number of marks
A	1	AO1	4
A	2	AO2	8
A	3	AO2	8
A	4	AO4	20
B	5	AO5, AO6	40

York Notes Practice Test One – Paper 2

Section	Question number	AO	Number of marks
A	1	AO1	2
A	2	AO1	2
A	3	AO1	8
A	4	AO2	12
A	5	AO3	16
B	6	AO5, AO6	40

York Notes Practice Test Two – Paper 2

Section	Question number	AO	Number of marks
A	1	AO1	4
A	2	AO1	8
A	3	AO2	12
A	4	AO3	16
B	5	AO5, AO6	40

PART TWO: YORK NOTES PRACTICE TEST ONE

Paper 1: Reading and writing imaginative/creative texts

Instructions

- Time allowed: 1 hour 45 minutes*
- The text material is printed within this practice paper. Please refer to this in your answers.
- Answer **all** questions.
- Answer the questions in the space provided, continuing onto a separate sheet if needed.
- Do all rough work in a notebook or on separate sheets of paper.
- You should **not** use a dictionary.

Information for candidates

- There are two sections: **Section A** (Reading) and **Section B** (Writing).
- Section A (Reading): 40 marks
- Section B (Writing): 40 marks
- The number of marks is given in brackets at the end of each question.

Advice

- Read each question carefully before you start to answer it.
- Check your answers if you have time at the end.

Some exam boards/organisations allow 2 hours for this paper.

Text A

An extract from Sons and Lovers *by D. H. Lawrence, 1913.*

In this extract William, the oldest son, who works in London, is expected home for Christmas.

He was coming at Christmas for five days. There had never been such preparations. Paul and Arthur scoured the land for holly and evergreens. Annie made the pretty paper hoops in the old-fashioned way. And there was unheard-of extravagance in the larder. Mrs. Morel made a big and magnificent cake. Then, feeling queenly, she showed Paul how to blanch almonds.

5 He skinned the long nuts reverently, counting them all, to see not one was lost. It was said that eggs whisked better in a cold place. So the boy stood in the scullery, where the temperature was nearly at freezing-point, and whisked and whisked, and flew in excitement to his mother as the white of egg grew stiffer and more snowy.

'Just look, mother! Isn't it lovely?'

10 And he balanced a bit on his nose, then blew it in the air.

'Now, don't waste it,' said the mother.

Everybody was mad with excitement. William was coming on Christmas Eve. Mrs. Morel surveyed her pantry. There was a big plum cake, and a rice cake, jam tarts, lemon tarts, and mince-pies – two enormous dishes. She was finishing cooking – Spanish tarts and cheese-

15 cakes. Everywhere was decorated. The kissing bunch of berried holly hung with bright and glittering things, spun slowly over Mrs. Morel's head as she trimmed her little tarts in the kitchen. A great fire roared. There was a scent of cooked pastry. He was due at seven o'clock, but he would be late. The three children had gone to meet him. She was alone. But at a quarter to seven Morel came in again. Neither wife nor husband spoke. He sat in his

20 armchair, quite awkward with excitement, and she quietly went on with her baking. Only by the careful way in which she did things could it be told how much moved she was. The clock ticked on.

'What time dost say he's coming?' Morel asked for the fifth time.

'The train gets in at half-past six,' she replied emphatically.

25 'Then he'll be here at ten past seven.'

'Eh, bless you, it'll be hours late on the Midland,' she said indifferently. But she hoped, by expecting him late, to bring him early. Morel went down the entry to look for him. Then he came back.

'Goodness, man!' she said. 'You're like an ill-sitting hen.'

30 'Hadna you better be gettin' him summat t' eat ready?' asked the father.

'There's plenty of time,' she answered.

'There's not so much as I can see on,' he answered, turning crossly in his chair. She began to clear her table.

The kettle was singing. They waited and waited.

35 Meantime the three children were on the platform at Sethley Bridge, on the Midland main line, two miles from home. They waited one hour. A train came – he was not there. Down the line the red and green lights shone. It was very dark and very cold.

'Ask him if the London train's come,' said Paul to Annie, when they saw a man in a tip cap.

'I'm not,' said Annie. 'You be quiet – he might send us off.'

40 But Paul was dying for the man to know they were expecting someone by the London train: it sounded so grand. Yet he was much too much scared of broaching any man, let alone one in a peaked cap, to dare to ask. The three children could scarcely go into the waiting-room for fear of being sent away, and for fear something should happen whilst they were off the platform. Still they waited in the dark and cold.

45 'It's an hour an' a half late,' said Arthur pathetically.

'Well,' said Annie, 'it's Christmas Eve.'

They all grew silent. He wasn't coming. They looked down the darkness of the railway. There was London! It seemed the utter-most of distance. They thought anything might happen if one came from London. They were all too troubled to talk. Cold, and unhappy, and silent,
50 they huddled together on the platform.

Turn over for Section A

Section A: Reading

Answer **all** questions in this section.
You are advised to spend about half the exam time on this section.

1 Read again the first part of the text, **lines 1 to 8.**

List **four** ways in which the children help their mother to prepare for William's arrival.

(4 marks)

1 _____

_____

2 _____

_____

3 _____

_____

4 _____

_____

2 Read from 'Neither husband nor wife spoke' in **line 19** to **line 33**.

What impressions does the writer give of Mr and Mrs Morel in these lines?

You could include the writer's choice of:

- words and phrases
- language features and techniques
- sentence forms.

You must refer to the text to support your answer.

(8 marks)

_____

_____

_____

_____

_____

_____

_____

❸ You now need to think about the **whole** of the text.

How does the writer use language and structure to show the change in mood as the text progresses?

You could write about:

- what the writer focuses your attention on at the beginning of the text
- how and why the writer changes this focus as the text develops
- relevant words and phrases, linguistic techniques and sentence forms.

(8 marks)

_____

_____

_____

_____

_____

_____

_____

_____

_____

_____

_____

_____

_____

_____

_____

_____

_____

_____

_____

_____

_____

_____

_____

_____

4 'In **lines 35 to 50** of this passage, the writer encourages readers to feel and share the children's emotions'.

To what extent do you agree with this view?

You should write about:

- your own impressions of the children's emotions as they are presented here, and in the passage as a whole
- how the writer has created these impressions.

(20 marks)

_____

_____

_____

_____

_____

_____

_____

_____

_____

_____

_____

_____

_____

_____

_____

_____

_____

_____

_____

_____

_____

_____

_____

_____

Section B: Writing

You are advised to spend about half the exam time on this section.
Write in full sentences.
You are reminded of the need to plan your answer.
You should leave enough time to check your work at the end.

5 Write a story about a time when you had to wait for someone to arrive. (Your story can be real or imagined.)

(40 marks)

_____

_____

_____

_____

_____

_____

_____

_____

_____

_____

_____

_____

_____

_____

_____

_____

_____

_____

_____

_____

END OF QUESTIONS

Paper 2: Reading and writing non-fiction texts

Instructions

- Time allowed: 1 hour 45 minutes*
- The text material is printed within this practice paper. Please refer to this in your answers.
- Answer **all** questions.
- Answer the questions in the space provided, continuing onto a separate sheet if needed.
- Do all rough work in a notebook or on separate sheets of paper.
- You should **not** use a dictionary.

Information for candidates

- There are two sections: **Section A** (Reading) and **Section B** (Writing).
- Section A (Reading): 40 marks
- Section B (Writing): 40 marks
- The number of marks is given in brackets at the end of each question.

Advice

- Read each question carefully before you start to answer it.
- Check your answers if you have time at the end.

Some exam boards/organisations allow 2 hours for this paper.

Text A

This text is an extract from an article written for The Guardian *by John Vidal to express his concerns about litter and flytipping in Britain.*

We are on the verge of a litter crisis

The Guardian, Thursday 25 February 2016
by John Vidal (theguardian.com)

The canal bank beside Northbrook Street near Birmingham city centre looks and smells like a tip. The grass is strewn with plastic cups, fag packets, cans, tins, wraps, cloth, papers, peel, bin liners, bags, butts and bottles. Builders have come in vans and flytipped waste, kids have graffitied the brickwork.

5   The canalside has been nominated by the public as one of the worst 'grotspots' in British cities and an army of volunteer litter pickers will descend on it and hundreds of other places in March in an attempt to tackle what has become known as the 'blight of Britain'.

For Chris, a retiree living in the nearby north Summerfield, the litter is offensive, depressing and incomprehensible. 'I have challenged people. You watch them eat their sandwiches and
10 then chuck the packaging away. "Hang on," I say. "I live here." "Oh I am sorry," they say. People know what they are doing is wrong but they think someone else pays the bills,' she says.

[…]

'I just don't understand people who litter. I have seen cars stop at traffic lights, a door open
15 and a used takeaway bag put on the road. What do you do? It's a culture. Perhaps it starts in schools.'

[…]

A recent Populus survey found that 90% of respondents consider litter to be a massive issue, with 81% saying that seeing litter makes them angry and frustrated.

20 It also found that 82% thought having litter on the streets encouraged other people to drop litter, and 93% said that littering shows a lack of respect for the environment. However, 61% of people said they would be afraid to confront people who drop litter.

'Rates of fast food littering and flytipping are on the rise and people find this really offensive. We are now on the verge of a crisis,' said Richard McIlwain, operations director of Keep
25 Britain Tidy.

'We seem to have more litter than anywhere else in the world. The risk is that over the next five years local authorities will come under even more financial pressure and will have to cut back on services further. If so, we will see environmental degradation across large areas of Britain and people's sense of wellbeing will decline.'

30 Around 2.25m pieces of litter are dropped on the streets of the UK every day. Thirty million tonnes of rubbish are collected from England's streets each year and it costs councils more than £1bn a year to clean up.

Hotspots include canals and verges but also motorways. The Highways Agency clears about 180,000 sacks of litter from motorways and A-roads alone. In 2013–14, local authorities dealt

35 with 852,000 flytipping incidents in England and Wales. These cost roughly £45m to clear up.

Text B

An extract from a letter addressed to the Editor of The Times *newspaper, by Professor Faraday.*

Observations on the Filth of the Thames

July 7, 1855

SIR,

I traversed this day by steam-boat the space between London and Hungerford Bridges between half-past one and two o'clock; it was low water, and I think the tide must have been
5   near the turn. The appearance and the smell of the water forced themselves at once on my attention. The whole of the river was an opaque pale brown fluid. (…)

The smell was very bad, and common to the whole of the water; it was the same as that which now comes up from the gully-holes[1] in the streets; the whole river was for the time a real sewer. Having just returned from out of the country air, I was, perhaps, more affected
10   by it than others; but I do not think I could have gone on to Lambeth or Chelsea, and I was glad to enter the streets for an atmosphere which, except near the sink-holes,[2] I found much sweeter than that on the river.

I have thought it a duty to record these facts that they may be brought to the attention of those who exercise power or have responsibility in relation to the condition of our river;
15   there is nothing figurative in the words I have employed, or any approach to exaggeration; they are the simple truth. If there be sufficient authority to remove a putrescent[3] pond from the neighbourhood of a few simple dwellings, surely the river which flows for so many miles through London ought not to be allowed to become a fermenting sewer.

The condition in which I saw the Thames may perhaps be considered as exceptional, but
20   it ought to be an impossible state, instead of which I fear it is rapidly becoming the general condition. If we neglect this subject, we cannot expect to do so with impunity;[4] nor ought we to be surprised if, ere many years are over, a hot season give us sad proof of the folly of our carelessness.

I am, Sir,
25   Your obedient servant,
M. FARADAY.
Royal Institution, July 7

Glossary

gully-holes[1] – where water comes out of the drains.
sink-holes[2] – holes in the ground (possibly a reference to the gully holes again).
putrescent[3] – rotting.
impunity[4] – freedom from punishment.

Section A: Reading

Answer **all** questions in this section.
You are advised to spend about half the exam time on this section.

❶ Refer to **Text A**, the article by John Vidal, **lines 1 to 4**. Identify two different ways in which the canal area has been spoilt.

(2 marks)

1 _____

_____

2 _____

_____

❷ Refer to **Text B**, Faraday's letter, **lines 1 to 9**. Give two quotations which show that he believes the River Thames is badly polluted.

(2 marks)

1 _____

_____

2 _____

_____

❸ Refer to **both** texts. According to these two writers, what are the main problems with the environments they describe?

(8 marks)

4 Refer only to **Text A**. How does John Vidal use persuasive language to make readers feel that litter is a significant problem in Britain?

(12 marks)

5 Both texts reveal the writers' feelings about the spoilt environments they are describing.

Compare the following:

- the writers' views about the spoilt environments
- the methods they use to get across their views or experiences.

You must use the text to support your comments and make it clear which text you are referring to.

(16 marks)

_____

_____

_____

_____

_____

_____

_____

_____

_____

_____

_____

_____

_____

_____

_____

_____

_____

_____

_____

_____

_____

_____

_____

_____

_____

Section B: Writing

You are advised to spend about half the exam time on this section.
Write in full sentences.
You are reminded of the need to plan your answer.
You should leave enough time to check your work at the end.

6 Your local council is keen to find ways to improve the environment.

Write the text of a speech to the council suggesting ways in which his might be done.

You could include:

- examples of environmental problems at the moment
- your ideas about how the situation could be improved.

(40 marks)

_____

_____

_____

_____

_____

_____

_____

_____

_____

_____

_____

_____

_____

_____

_____

_____

_____

_____

_____

_____

END OF QUESTIONS

Answers and sample responses

Paper 1: Section A

❶ (AO1)

Any four or more answers from the following:

- Paul and Arthur searched for 'holly and evergreens'.
- Annie made decorations 'the old-fashioned way', using 'pretty paper hoops'.
- Paul learned how to blanch almonds.
- Paul skinned the almonds 'reverently'.
- Paul counted all the almonds carefully, 'to see not one was lost'.
- Paul whisked the eggs in the freezing scullery.
- He 'whisked and whisked' the eggs until they were stiff and fluffy.

❷ (AO2)

Possible answers

- Both parents seem wrapped up in their own thoughts, at the start of this extract, since neither of them speak. It is likely that they are both thinking about William's arrival.
- Lawrence's short sentence 'The clock ticked on' could imply that both Mr and Mrs Morel are acutely aware of the clock because they are waiting to see their son.
- Lawrence draws attention to the differences between Mr and Mrs Morel by showing us that Mr Morel is restless and agitated but (on the surface) Mrs Morel seems calm.
- Mr Morel is described as being 'awkward with excitement'. The adjective 'awkward' implies that waiting around makes him feel uncomfortable.
- Lawrence implies that Mr Morel is restless when he tells us 'Morel went down the entry to look for him. Then he came back.' The second sentence is shorter than the first which could suggest disappointment or anti-climax.
- Lawrence indicates that Morel repeats himself: 'What time dost say he's coming?' Morel asked for the fifth time.' The writer's use of the word 'fifth' suggests that Morel had asked the question far too often due to his agitated state.
- Morel tells his wife that she should prepare a meal. When she does not respond to this suggestion he turns away 'crossly'. The adverb 'crossly' suggests that he is sulking or in a bad mood.
- On the surface Mrs Morel is calmer and quieter than her husband. However, Lawrence shares some of her thinking with his readers to show this is not true.
- The writer tells us she was baking 'quietly' and this adverb implies that she was silent as she worked. However, she is also 'careful' in her work. The adjective 'careful' suggests that she is also meticulous, which may be covering up her hidden excitement.
- Lawrence also tells us that Mrs Morel was 'moved', which implies that she is responding emotionally to the situation.
- Mrs Morel replies 'indifferently'. This adverb suggests that she is trying to sound as if she does not care about William's arrival.
- She uses a simile when she tells Mr Morel, 'You're like an ill-sitting hen'. This shows that she has noticed his restlessness and may be annoyed by it.
- At the end of this extract she begins to clear the table even though she has claimed there is 'plenty of time', so we could infer that she is more excited than she appears to be on the surface.

Sample student responses

Mid Level: A clear understanding of language, with relevant details, effects explained and accurate terminology. For example:

Mr and Mrs Morel behave very differently but I think they have some feelings in common. At the start of this extract neither of them 'spoke', which makes me think they are both secretly thinking about William. Later Mr Morel begins asking his wife questions. He asks, 'What time dost say he's coming?' five times. If you ask something that many times you must be very concerned about it. Morel also goes out to look for his son and then comes back, which tells me his search was all for nothing. It seems as if he can't settle down because he sat in his chair 'quite awkward with excitement'. The use of the noun 'excitement' shows how much he wanted his son to arrive.

I think Mrs Morel is probably excited too but she hides her real feelings. She carries on baking 'quietly' and this adverb suggests her behaviour is still and calm, not restless like her husband's. I think she is excited because she is 'moved', which means she is feeling emotional. I don't think Mr Morel is aware of his wife's thoughts, but the writer tells us about these so we see her inner excitement. At the end of the extract she makes Morel cross by saying there is 'plenty of time' to make a meal. However, she does begin to prepare the table which may imply that she is actually as excited as he is but she holds it inside more.

Higher Level: Detailed and perceptive understanding of language with very well-chosen details, analysis of the effects of the writer's choices and sophisticated use of terminology. For example:

The opening of this extract suggests that, when Mr Morel returns from work, the couple are both preoccupied by their own thoughts since neither of them 'spoke'. Since this passage is about waiting for William, we might presume that they are both contemplating his imminent arrival. This impression is reinforced by Lawrence's use of the short, sharp sentence 'The clock ticked on.' Here the words 'ticked on' imply a continual, repetitive sound. It is likely that both parents are highly aware of this ticking and that the writer is using it to represent their extended waiting time. Lawrence also chooses to place this sentence about the clock at the end of a paragraph so the words 'ticked on' linger in the reader's mind for longer than they would if this sentence was placed elsewhere. Readers might infer that the sound of the clock stayed in the Morels' minds in the same way.

Although both Morels seem to be waiting hopefully, Lawrence uses a number of techniques to reveal their differences. Mr Morel appears to find the waiting period particularly difficult since he is 'awkward with excitement' in his chair. The use of the adjective 'awkward' implies that he is uncomfortable, while the noun 'excitement' clearly highlights his eager anticipation. Morel also seems restless as we are told that he 'went down the entry to look for him. Then he came back.' The second, shorter sentence 'Then he came back' conveys disappointment since it seems like an anti-climax after the previous longer one where he is eagerly looking out for his son. Mr Morel also asks his wife when William will arrive for the 'fifth time'. The writer's use of 'fifth' suggests that Morel repeats the same question far more often than necessary. Morel also suggests that his wife should be preparing William's meal, even though she is already baking, and when her reply doesn't satisfy him he turns 'crossly' in his chair. Here the use of the adverb 'crossly' suggests that he is unhappy about his wife's response or perhaps he is sulking as a child would.

Mrs Morel answers her husband's question about William's arrival 'indifferently'. The use of this adverb suggests that she is acting as if she does not care, but perhaps Lawrence allows enough glimpses of her real feelings for readers to infer that she does. In addition, she seems irritated when she tells her husband, 'You're like an ill-sitting hen'. This simile refers to his obvious restlessness since an ill-sitting hen would be unsettled and not sitting calmly on the nest. However, despite her apparent indifference, Mrs Morel seems to respond to her husband's suggestion that she should prepare the meal because soon after this 'She began to clear the table'. Therefore, while Mr and Mrs Morel are both waiting for William, Mrs Morel contains her emotions but her husband does not.

❸ (AO2)

Possible answers

- This extract begins with excited anticipation of William's arrival and ends with unhappiness and disappointment.
- Lawrence uses topic sentences to highlight the family's feelings. For example, the initial excitement is shown in the first two lines where Lawrence reveals that 'He was coming … for five days' and that 'There had never been such preparations'. These lines deliberately establish both William's imminent return and the family's joy about this.
- Lawrence then focuses on significant details such as the 'big and magnificent cake' and Paul whisking the eggs. The adjectives 'big' and 'magnificent' are used to depict the splendour of the cake and the fluffy eggs are a symbol for Paul's rising excitement.
- Another topic sentence reinforces the idea of joyful anticipation when we are told 'Everybody was mad with excitement'.
- Lawrence provides more information about the Morel family's preparations by telling us about the food Mrs Morel had cooked: 'There was a big plum cake, and a rice cake, jam tarts, lemon tarts, and mince-pies – two enormous dishes.' This long list, with 'two enormous dishes' separated from the rest of the sentence for emphasis, is used to convey extravagance.
- Lawrence enhances the happy mood by describing how the 'berried holly hung with bright and glittering things'. Here both the red berries and the brightness of the ornaments which 'swung slowly over Mrs. Morel's head' suggest joy.
- Lawrence makes use of the senses when he describes a great fire which 'roared' and the 'scent' of cooked pastry. The adjective 'great' and the verb 'roared' convey an enormous fire, while the delicious smell of cooking suggests a pleasant atmosphere.
- The focus then shifts to an episode where the parents are waiting at home for William. Here the mood becomes uncomfortable and tense. Mr Morel is 'awkward with excitement' and Mrs Morel says very little. Here Mr Morel's feelings are displayed outwardly whilst Mrs Morel's are mostly hidden within.
- At the end of this section, Lawrence says, 'The kettle was singing. They waited and waited.' These sentences are powerful as the verb 'waited' is repeated to suggest an extended period of time passing. The singing kettle shows that they were ready to serve tea. However, the verb 'singing' is often used to show happiness so this mirrors their earlier joy.

- Lawrence shifts focus to the children at the station. At this stage the mood gradually changes from excitement to despair.
- Darkness is used as a symbol of dying hope and Lawrence suggests this by beginning the scene with red and green lights further down the railway (reflecting the children's excitement) and then changing this to 'the darkness of the railway' later on.
- Near the end of the passage, Lawrence suggests 'He wasn't coming', implying that all the preparations were for nothing. The children are left 'Cold, and unhappy, and silent' and 'huddled together on the platform'. The mood here is sad and dark.

Sample student responses

Mid Level: A clear understanding of language and structural features with a range of relevant examples referred to using accurate terminology. For example:

In this passage the mood starts off joyful and ends up miserable. Lawrence begins with the eager preparations in and around the family home and ends up with the three children standing miserably on the station.

At the beginning of this piece he immediately tells us that William is due to arrive and that the family are getting ready. The mood here is joyful. Initially Mrs Morel does a lot of baking. We are told about the 'big plum cake' and the 'enormous dishes'. The words 'big' and 'enormous' also suggest extravagance and a happy mood.

In the second section of this passage, Lawrence shows us the parents waiting at home. Here the mood is not so joyful and the parents seem tense. When Mr Morel comes home from work his wife says he is 'like an ill-sitting hen', which shows us he is restless. Mrs Morel keeps busy because she does not want to reveal her true feelings.

After this section, the writer completely shifts focus to describe the three children waiting at the station. At first they are proud and excited to be waiting for a London train but after an hour the mood changes and finally Lawrence says they are 'cold, unhappy and silent', which is very different from how they were feeling earlier when Paul was happily whisking eggs. In this ending the writer is indicating how the mood has changed and I think the writer's references to darkness show this because darkness is sometimes linked to death and sorrow.

Higher Level: Detailed and perceptive understanding of language and structural features with a very well-chosen range of examples and analysis of the effects of these features using sophisticated terminology. For example:

The mood portrayed in this piece gradually changes from eager anticipation to deep disappointment. The structure of Lawrence's writing reflects this mood shift since the opening takes place in and around the warm family home whilst the ending is set at a cold, dark station.

The family's feelings are often highlighted in Lawrence's carefully chosen topic sentences. In the first two lines readers are informed that 'He was coming ... for five days' and 'There had never been such preparations'. These lines deliberately establish the subject of William's arrival. Initially the writer's focus is on significant details, such as Mrs Morel's 'big and magnificent cake', where the adjectives 'big' and 'magnificent' are used to depict the splendour of her masterpiece.

During this initial, joyful episode, Lawrence also describes Paul eagerly whisking the eggs, which froth up to reflect his bubbling excitement. A further topic sentence reinforces the family's excited mood when the second paragraph begins 'Everybody was mad with excitement'. The noun 'excitement' conveys both eagerness and enthusiasm.

In addition, Lawrence reveals more about the joyful preparations. He tells us that Mrs Morel feels like a 'queen' in the kitchen, which suggests that her baking makes her feel empowered. He then goes on to list all the food that she has cooked to convey abundance. Lawrence enhances this feeling by referring to the 'berried holly hung with bright and glittering things'. Here readers are encouraged to imagine the bright red berries covered in shining ornaments which 'swung slowly over Mrs. Morel's head'. The alliteration in 'swung slowly' reflects the movement of this decoration, which may remind readers of a large, glittering ball swinging above a dance hall, adding to the sense of excitement.

In order to develop his descriptions of this joyful mood, Lawrence also makes use of the senses when he refers to the great fire which 'roared' and the 'scent' of cooked pastry. The combination of the adjective 'great' and the verb 'roared' is used effectively to convey the sound of an enormous fire burning. His reference to the smell of pastry invites readers to imagine that they too can breathe in this delicious scent. In addition, the warmth in this episode deliberately contrasts with the cold station at the end of this passage.

After this initial episode of delightful anticipation, Lawrence changes focus to depict the parents waiting at home. Here the mood seems more tense and uncomfortable as Mr Morel is restless and 'awkward with excitement', indicating that he feels restless. Mrs Morel is quiet and 'careful'.

After he has given readers an impression of Mr and Mrs Morel, Lawrence says, 'The kettle was singing. They waited and waited.' Here the writer conveys a great deal in a few words. The repetition of the verb 'waited' implies that the interim period between preparing for William and his arrival seems unending, whilst the fact that the kettle is singing suggests that the couple are poised and ready to serve tea at any moment. However, the verb 'singing' also echoes the earlier, more joyful, mood because 'singing' is a verb associated with happiness.

Next, Lawrence shifts focus to describe the children at the station. The mood in this last episode changes gradually from excitement to despair. Initially Paul feels keen to tell somebody that they are meeting William from the London train because it 'sounded so grand'. This shows that he thinks their situation is special, but Annie brings him down to earth when she reminds him that if they draw attention to themselves they may be sent home.

The mood darkens after the three children see a train arrive and leave without William alighting. This deflated mood is then further highlighted when Lawrence repeats the word 'dark'. Here the 'dark' is used to symbolise a loss of hope and Lawrence develops this by also referring to 'the darkness of the railway' in his final paragraph.

As the last lights on the railway track are lost, readers are left to picture the children 'Cold, and unhappy, and silent' and 'huddled together on the platform'. This ending shows how their eager anticipation has been replaced by unhappiness and freezing conditions. The use of the word 'huddled' implies that the children were standing close together for warmth but we could infer that they were also seeking some kind of comfort. The ending seems like a sad anti-climax after all the previous, joyful anticipation.

4 (AO4)

Possible answers

- Lawrence tells us the most about Paul's feelings so some readers may find it easiest to relate to his emotions.
- Arthur's emotions are not revealed as directly so he is more difficult to empathise with. He only says, 'It's an hour an' a half late'. These words suggest he is unhappy at the station.
- Arthur speaks 'pathetically'. The word 'pathetic' is sometimes used to convey unhappiness or

neediness. This may give readers the impression that Arthur is whinging, which would not encourage them to empathise with him.

- Annie seems to be in charge of the other children as she tells Paul, 'You be quiet – he might send us off'. Readers may be able to relate to her by imagining how difficult it is for her to control her brothers when she also felt excited.
- Earlier on Annie makes paper hoops 'the old-fashioned way'. This could be a slow process and suggests that she does it because she loves William. This makes her seem careful and caring. These may be traits that readers can understand and admire.
- On the station Paul is 'dying for the man to know they were expecting someone by the London train' because 'it sounded so grand'. This suggests that he is proud of being there to meet his brother. At that time, a life in London would have seemed very different from everyday reality so readers may understand why Paul finds William's arrival so 'grand'.
- Paul seems to have mixed feelings whilst he is at the station. He wants to find out information about the London train but we are also told that 'he was much too scared of broaching any man, let alone one in a peaked cap'. The word 'scared' shows that he is in awe of the official's authority (symbolised by the peaked cap). Paul's emotions are understandable here as he is in an unfamiliar situation.
- Earlier on in the text Paul 'flew in excitement' when the eggs grew stiffer and then 'balanced a bit on his nose'. Such details make his feelings easy to empathise with because his childish actions clearly indicate his joy.
- Some of the children's emotions are shown by grouping them together. For example, they all waited together for an hour before 'A train came – he was not there.' This train would have momentarily raised the children's hopes until they discovered that William was 'not there'. Most readers would be able to relate to this.
- Lawrence helps readers to understand the children's emotions when he uses light to symbolise their emotions in the lines: 'Down the line the red and green lights shone' and 'They looked down the darkness of the railway'. The lights represent hopes that are strong at first and then fade.
- By the end of the extract the children are 'Cold, and unhappy, and silent' and 'huddled together on the platform'. After their excited anticipation in the first half of the text such a dejected feeling is easy to relate to.

Sample student responses

Mid Level: A clear and relevant evaluation, which uses a range of textual details to evaluate the effect(s) on the reader. This answer shows a clear understanding of the writer's methods and a relevant response to the statement in the question. For example:

I don't agree completely with the statement as I don't feel all the children's emotions. I think I only connect to some of them. However, I can imagine how they must feel waiting on the station for William. The writer tells us that the children 'waited in the dark and cold'. When he repeats 'cold' and 'dark' I can imagine their unhappy situation and share some of their feelings.

The writer does not reveal as many of Annie's and Arthur's feelings as Paul's. We are told about them when they are in the group of cold, sad children at the station but we don't learn much else about them. Paul is the easiest to relate to as he is silly in the kitchen when he mucks about putting whisked eggs on his nose. I think he does this because he is so excited.

Paul seems to have mixed feelings as, even though he is fearful at the station, he is also proud to be collecting William when he thinks, 'they were expecting someone by the London train: it sounded so grand'. However, his excitement in the kitchen and his changing emotions on the platform are easy to imagine. Therefore I share some of the children's feelings but I relate more to Paul's than Annie's or Arthur's because vivid details like the egg whisking make him seem more real.

Higher Level: Shows perceptive and detailed evaluation using a very well-chosen range of textual details to evaluate the effect(s) on the reader. This answer shows perceptive understanding of the writer's methods and develops a convincing and critical response to the statement in the question. For example:

I agree with this statement to a certain extent but I would argue that it is easiest to 'feel' Paul's emotions because we are told the most about his feelings.

I find it most difficult to share Arthur's emotions. This is because during the episode at the station he only speaks a few words: 'It's an hour an' a half late'. These words indicate his impatience and anxiety. We are also told that he speaks 'pathetically', a word sometimes used to convey unhappiness. From this word I also get the impression that he may be a needy, whinging child, although there is little evidence to support this. However, for the rest of this extract, he is grouped together with the others as one of the 'children'. For this reason, I do not really feel his emotions. Even when I review the entire passage, I only discover slightly more about Arthur.

Lawrence tells his readers that Arthur went with Paul to find holly and evergreens. I presume that he was excited at this time but I do not learn enough about him to empathise with his emotions.

Annie is somewhat easier to understand. She is probably the eldest child since Paul defers to her when she refuses to talk to a station official. She tells him, 'You be quiet – he might send us off'. The reader might therefore infer that she wants to remain in control of the other children. I do understand how difficult it would be for a young girl to control two excited siblings when her own emotions may also be in turmoil.

Lawrence reveals Paul's emotions in far more detail. On the station he is 'dying for the man to know they were expecting someone by the London train' because 'it sounded so grand'. This suggests that he felt a real sense of importance. Sadly, these positive feelings are quickly deflated when we are told that 'he was much too scared of broaching any man, let alone one in a peaked cap'. The word 'scared' shows that he is afraid of the man's authority (symbolised by the peaked cap). On the other hand, his excitable nature is revealed at the start of the text where he tries to help his mother in the kitchen but 'flew in excitement' when the eggs grew stiffer and then 'balanced a bit on his nose'. This implies that he sometimes acts immaturely, but this egg whisking episode and his fear on the station are both endearing. Such details make his feelings easy to empathise with.

As well as these individual characteristics, the children's emotions are conveyed by grouping them together. For example, they all waited together for an hour before 'A train came – he was not there.' The brief pause in the middle of this sentence reflects the short time when the train stopped at the station. This would have momentarily raised the children's expectations until they discovered he was 'not there'. Lawrence also uses light to symbolise their emotions when he writes, 'Down the line the red and green lights shone'. These lights represent the children's hope. However, later we are told, 'They looked down the darkness of the railway', suggesting that their hope has faded and their emotions have changed. This use of darkness and light to reflect changes of feeling helps readers to relate to them.

Near the end of the extract the children are 'Cold, and unhappy, and silent' and 'huddled together on the platform'. This description suggests that they moved together to seek warmth and comfort. I can imagine their feelings at this time since I believe they are deeply disappointed. However, overall, I find Paul's feelings the easiest to relate to as the other two children are portrayed in less detail. Therefore, I can't fully agree with the statement in this question.

Paper 1: Section B

❺ (AO5) (AO6)

Sample student responses

Lower Level: Sometimes matched to purpose and audience. There is an attempt to use a varied vocabulary and some linguistic devices. At times the writing is clear and contains linked, relevant ideas with occasional variety in sentence structures. Some of the grammar and spelling is correct. For example:

> 'They went' is used to link two sentences in succession

> The grammar is incorrect; this should say 'They were'

> Too many sentences begin with 'They'

> This is not a full sentence

> There are too many short sentences in this section

> Student has omitted to include speech marks here, which makes the sense unclear

> Informal/incorrect: this should be 'really bad', using an adverb rather than an adjective to describe the verb 'feeling', but it would be better to use something less colloquial, e.g. 'terrible'

> This ends rather abruptly

Imran told Rory he had heard that the manager of the England football was renting a house in their village. They went to get his autograph on footballs. They went to wait near the house until he appeared. They arrived at eight in the morning. Then it was ten and they was still waiting.

'I'm getting bored,' said Rory.

'Let's try some high kicks,' said Imran. He had a go.

The ball flew high. It was a great kick. His best ever. Imran grinned.

'Just look at that!' he told Rory. 'That takes skill!'

The ball flew higher. Imran smiled again but Rory did not.

'You idiot,' he said. 'That ball is going over the fence!' They both watched the ball. Rory was right. It went over the fence. Then it fell. It landed in the manager's garden.

'Go and get it back,' snapped Rory. 'We need him to sign it.'

Imran looked around. The coast was clear. He could see the ball in the garden. He started to climb the fence.

A voice shouted 'Hey you!' The manager came running out of the house. 'Get off that fence!' Imran jumped down at once. 'I'm sorry,' he said.

Did you kick this ball into the garden? Imran looked down. Yes, he said.

The man opened the gate and let the boys in. They stood before him feeling real bad.

'Do you know what I think?' the man asked.

The boys shook their heads.

'That was a great kick,' said the manager. 'And I've watched you both playing football from my window.'

'Thanks,' said Imran.

'I am doing some work with the England youth development squad,' said the manager. 'I would like you both to have a trial.' The boys were so happy that they almost forgot about the autographs.

When they remembered, the manager signed their footballs. He also took their phone numbers then said, 'Now go away. No more waiting outside.' He went back inside.

Mid Level: This answer is generally well matched to purpose and audience. The vocabulary is chosen for effect and includes some sophisticated word choices. It also uses linguistic devices successfully. The writing is engaging and it contains a range of clear, connected ideas. A variety of sentence forms are used for effect. Grammar, punctuation and spelling (including the spelling of complex words) are all good. For example:

> *I was going out with Simon to a party at one of the best nightclubs in town. It was so exciting. It took me all afternoon to get ready because I longed to look perfect. After showering and drying my hair, I climbed in and out of at least fifteen different outfits before picking one.*
>
> *At last I was ready, wearing my black jeans and a new* sparkly silver *top. My nail varnish shone with silver sprinkles and not a scratch or bubble could be seen on any of the nails.*
>
> *However, my good mood plunged into despair when Simon was very, very late. He should have picked me up at seven but there was no sign of him. It was nearly eight. The party would have started without us.*
>
> *Should I give up? Should I go on my own? Should I ask Dad for a lift? When I tried to ring Simon, his mobile was off and if I sent texts he did not reply.*
>
> *I walked to the mirror and brushed my blonde hair again. Then I added more mascara to my lashes.* Where was he? Why was I waiting?
>
> *My boyfriend had been* acting odd *all week. He had been really quiet. Perhaps he liked someone else? I imagined Simon with another girl at the party. Perhaps he had forgotten me?*
>
> *I thought about his blue eyes and wide smile. How could he do this to me and where was he now? How long could I go on waiting?*
>
> *I started to cry. My mascara ran down my face. Simon was never late. He must have met another girl. That would explain everything.*
>
> *I put my head in my hands and I cried and cried. Then at nine o'clock the doorbell rang. Could it be him at last? I went to the door, still crying. When I opened it Simon was there. He looked very pale. We stared at each other, then he spoke.*
>
> *'My Gran had a heart attack,' he said. 'I've been at the hospital waiting for news but now they've told us she's going to pull through.'*
>
> *I gave him a big hug because finally I understood everything.*

Annotations:

- Use of alliteration
- Use of pattern of three and rhetorical questions
- The use of short questions builds tension
- Incorrect: an adjective ('odd') is used to describe a verb ('acting'); the adverb should be used: 'acting oddly'
- This and the two previous paragraphs would be better combined or developed

Overall comment: This answer would benefit from a more sophisticated vocabulary

Higher Level: This answer is confidently matched to purpose and audience. The vocabulary is extensive and ambitious. The writing is compelling and fluently linked, using a full range of sentence forms for effect. Grammar, punctuation and spelling (including the spelling of ambitious vocabulary) are all excellent. For example:

Establishes the setting well

The heavy wooden door closed behind me with a clatter as I peered through my glasses at the imposing grandeur of the hallway. A few beams of light fell from narrow windows. Burgundy walls displayed carefully arranged portraits where grim strangers appraised me through dead eyes.

I held my breath for a moment, struggling to regain my composure as an angular figure in grey closed in on me. She was tall, thin and moving briskly down the corridor, her high-heels click-clicking against the polished marble floor. When she reached me, she extended her hand theatrically like the star of a Victorian melodrama.

Use of onomatopoeia: we can hear the sound of the shoes in 'click-clicking'

Use of simile

'I am Petunia Stapleton,' she told me. 'I own this hotel … I presume you are here regarding the weekend waitressing position,' she added, after a brief handshake.

'Yes, that's right,' I stuttered, hoping that she hadn't noticed my sweaty palm. 'I am Diana Lee.'

'Then, follow me, Miss Lee,' she instructed. 'I will take you to the waiting room.'

My flat black shoes followed her sharp heels as she made her way back down the corridor. Her heels clicked on, eventually we reached an oak-panelled door.

She turned the brass doorknob, saying, 'Wait in here, please.' I followed her into what appeared to be a drawing room. 'I am concluding my discussions with the last candidate,' continued Mrs Stapleton. 'There is a jug of water on the side table if you feel thirsty. I trust you will be comfortable waiting here.'

'Quite comfortable, thank you.'

'Good, good,' she said, 'I will be back in a while to conduct your interview.'

When she had gone, I wondered what she meant by 'a while'. I would have preferred not to have to wait at all as I knew that the longer she took, the more nervous I would become. However, thirty minutes later I was still waiting.

I poured myself a glass of iced water to soothe my dry throat. Then I paced around the room sipping it slowly. Still nothing … Where on earth was she?

Use of alliteration

There were great, green curtains draped around the windows. I peered out at an autumnal lawn where wind toyed with dead leaves. An elderly man entered the scene and started gathering these leaves into piles. His work seemed futile for with every gust of wind it was undone.

I longed for another glass of iced water, but this would mean an untimely trip to the toilet. The moment I left the room, she would be sure to reappear only to find me missing. I watched the gardener sweeping up the same pile of leaves for the third time.

Forty-five minutes passed and Mrs Stapleton still had not returned. I had had enough. I approached the door with new determination. And, of course, even as my clammy fingers closed around the doorknob, there she was, almost nose to nose with me, in the doorway.

'Running away, dear?' she asked almost cheerfully.

Meekly, I turned back to my chair. 'I will conduct the interview here,' she said, 'to avoid further delay. I'm afraid I left you waiting rather longer than I expected. You see, it turned out that the last candidate was acquainted with an old friend of mine, Miss Gladys Stevens. We got caught up discussing Gladys's recipe for lemon cake.'

Now I knew that my waiting had been in vain! When Mrs Stapleton asked her first question, I couldn't come up with any answer. Outside the gardener had given up on the leaves. For a moment he stood there, admitting defeat, and then he picked up his barrow and wheeled it away empty.

The gardener and the leaves are used to symbolise Diana's situation

Paper 2: Section A

❶ (AO1)

Any two or more answers from the following:

- Building waste has been 'flytipped'.
- There is graffiti on 'the brickwork'.
- People have abandoned items from their picnics: like peel, bottles, plastic cups and food wrappers.
- Smokers have littered the area with cigarette packets and butts.

❷ (AO1)

Any two or more answers from the following:
- 'The appearance and the smell of the water forced themselves at once on my attention.'
- 'The whole of the river was an opaque pale brown fluid.'
- 'The smell was very bad, and common to the whole of the water'
- 'the whole river was for the time a real sewer'

❸ (AO1)

Possible answers

Main problems identified in Text A by John Vidal

- Vidal refers to the problem of litter in several contexts, such as canal banks and motorways.
- He calls the canalsides 'the worst "grotspots" in British cities'.
- He claims that the canal bank 'looks and smells like a tip'.
- The grass is 'strewn' with litter and various dumped items.
- Building waste has been 'flytipped'.
- There is graffiti on 'the brickwork'.
- Smokers drop 'fag packets' and butts.
- People eat takeaways and picnics then drop their peel, drink containers and wrappings.
- Roads get more polluted every time 'a door opens and a used takeaway bag (is) put on the road'.
- Figures indicate the situation is getting worse and heading for a crisis.

Main problems identified in Text B by Faraday

- Faraday focuses on the problem of pollution in the River Thames.
- He claims that the Thames smells 'very bad'.
- The summer heat makes the unpleasant smell even worse.
- The river could become a 'fermenting sewer'.
- The water is filthy and consists of 'opaque pale brown fluid'.
- He has 'to enter the streets' to escape from the smell of the river.

- He feels that the current situation will become the norm unless action is taken.

Sample student responses

Mid Level: A clear synthesis and interpretation of both texts, using relevant details and inferences and showing the differences between texts. For example:

These two writers both identify problems with the environments they are describing. Faraday believes that the River Thames smells 'very bad' and Vidal says the canal bank 'looks and smells like a tip'. Vidal also explains why this area looks bad. He claims the mess is due to kids doing graffiti, men flytipping and other people dropping a load of rubbish without using bins. It seems that the Thames does not look good either as Faraday writes about the water being 'brown' and 'opaque' and later on he claims it could become a 'fermenting sewer' full of waste matter.

Both the writers think the problems may be getting worse. Faraday really hopes that the bad condition of the Thames is 'exceptional' but fears it will become normal if 'we neglect this subject'. Vidal uses experts to show that litter and flytipping are increasing because people are careless and do silly things like dropping their takeaway packets out of car doors.

I think Faraday cares most about the state of the Thames but Vidal is worried about rubbish in several different locations such as canals, verges and motorways. Both writers want to get other people to think more about environmental concerns, which is why they describe the main problems they see.

Higher Level: A perceptive synthesis and interpretation of both texts. Well-chosen textual details are used effectively. Perceptive inferences are made from both texts, showing the differences between them: For example:

Both Vidal and Faraday believe their environments are being spoilt and that the waterways are in a terrible condition. Faraday refers to the repulsive condition of the River Thames, whilst Vidal describes untidy canal banks and claims that such areas are 'the worst "grotspots" in British cities'. In describing their environments both writers highlight foul smells. Vidal claims that the canal bank 'looks and smells like a tip' whilst Faraday states that the Thames smells 'very bad'. Similarly, both writers are also concerned about what they see. Vidal observes that the grass around the canal is 'strewn with' an assortment of litter, including food and drink containers, cigarette butts and bin liners. He also mentions flytipping and graffiti on the brickwork. Meanwhile, Faraday refers to the filthy appearance of the 'opaque pale brown' water in the polluted River Thames.

Vidal draws attention to the roads and Faraday mentions streets but their messages about these are very different. Vidal suggests that roads and motorways are being spoilt by careless drivers who don't think before they put another 'used takeaway bag' on the road. On the other hand, Faraday compares the streets favourably with the river when he writes that he is 'glad to enter the streets' because the air there is 'much sweeter than that on the river'. Therefore he describes the streets quite favourably in order to draw attention to the poor air quality around the Thames.

Faraday focuses on one main problem area: the River Thames. In contrast, Vidal considers problems in a wider range of contexts. His focus shifts from the canal banks to the roads. In addition, Vidal identifies a number of different problems, including litter, flytipping and graffiti, whilst Faraday focuses all his attention on the pollution of the Thames. However, it is clear that both these writers are highly concerned about the environmental problems in the areas they are describing and that they seek to bring these problems to the public's attention.

4 (AO2)

Possible answers

- John Vidal uses a number of persuasive techniques to convey his message that litter is a significant problem in Britain.
- His headline states that 'We are on the verge of a litter crisis', which suggests imminent disaster. The word 'verge' implies that the country is about to plunge into disaster whilst 'crisis' suggests a calamity. This headline is designed to make readers feel anxious and encourage them to continue reading.
- Vidal uses the senses of sight and smell to engage his readers: 'looks and smells like a tip'. These words present a grim picture of the canal banks because a tip is unpleasant.
- To indicate how much rubbish there is by the canal, Vidal uses the technique of listing. He lists many discarded items and these don't arise from one source. It is likely that 'peel' and 'plastic cups' may have been left by picnickers, but 'fag packets' and 'butts' could have been dropped by smokers.
- Vidal uses alliteration at the end of his list in the words 'bin liners, bags, butts and bottles'. This alliteration makes these words linger for longer in readers' minds, drawing further attention to the rubbish.
- Vidal does not just rely on his own voice as he also uses a number of other voices to make his article even more persuasive.

- Chris, 'a retiree living in the nearby north Summerfield', is used to indicate that ordinary people share Vidal's environmental concerns.
- Vidal uses a pattern of three when he states that Chris finds the litter 'offensive, depressing and incomprehensible'. These words suggest that the litter has upset Chris and that it may be mentally distressing.
- Vidal refers to a Populus survey which found that '90% of respondents consider litter to be a massive issue'. By using this figure from a national organisation Vidal adds authority to his own views.
- Vidal quotes Richard McIlwain from Keep Britain Tidy. McIlwain's statement is used to paint a picture of a terrible future where 'we will see environmental degradation across large areas of Britain'. These words support Vidal's title and enhance his view that the country is on the edge of calamity.
- Vidal also tells us that in one year the Highways Agency dealt with '852,000 flytipping incidents in England and Wales'. This large number also implies Britain's litter problem is extensive.
- In this article Vidal begins with his own perspective, then introduces authoritative voices to support his. This adds power to his viewpoint.

Sample student responses

Mid Level: A clear understanding of language with relevant details, effects explained and accurate use of terminology. For example:

Vidal thinks litter is a significant problem and he wants to make his readers feel the same way. He convinces them by using a range of persuasive techniques. He tells us that the canal bank is a 'tip' because there is so much mess there. This sounds shocking. He also persuades us by using a big list of twelve items of rubbish: 'plastic cups, fag packets, cans, tins, wraps, cloth, papers, peel, bin liners, bags, butts and bottles'. This long list makes me imagine all kinds of rubbish lying around. It may persuade readers to understand how he feels and to take action.

Then he quotes other sources, starting with a retiree called Chris, to back up his views. Chris finds the litter 'offensive' and 'depressing', so we feel sorry for her. It sounds like the litter has really upset Chris. Here Vidal seems to say that litter can make people miserable. This could also persuade readers to feel guilty about dropping it.

Vidal refers to a number of experts in his article. Their words make the article persuasive because they represent authority and provide numbers to support

Vidal's idea of there being a lot of litter. For example, he explains that a Populus survey stated that 81% of people said 'that seeing litter makes them angry and frustrated'. This is a bit like Chris's point. It seems as if litter has an impact on people's feelings. I guess the point is that if we are surrounded by litter then it will get us all down.

Higher Level: A detailed and perceptive understanding of language with relevant details, effects explained and sophisticated and accurate use of terminology. For example:

John Vidal clearly wants to convince readers that litter is a significant problem in Britain. Throughout his article he uses persuasive techniques in order to share his feelings.

His headline, 'We are on the verge of a litter crisis', suggests imminent disaster. The word 'verge' implies that the country has reached a tipping point whilst 'crisis' suggests catastrophe or calamity. Therefore, the overall effect of the headline is to make readers feel anxious and encourage them to read on.

Initially, Vidal expresses his own views about litter in his area. He uses a powerful phrase which draws on the senses of sight and smell to engage his readers: 'looks and smells like a tip'. These words present a grim picture of the canal banks, which is enhanced when Vidal uses the technique of listing various items of litter. Vidal also uses alliteration at the end of his list when he refers to 'bin liners, bags, butts and bottles'. This alliteration makes the list linger even longer in readers' minds.

Once the writer has presented his own viewpoint, he draws on other voices in order to make his article even more persuasive. The witness statement from Chris, 'a retiree', is used to indicate that members of the public share Vidal's environmental concerns. Vidal uses a pattern of three to describe Chris's feelings about the litter: 'offensive, depressing and incomprehensible'. These words suggest that the litter has changed Chris's emotions. Here Vidal is subtly inferring that litter can cause mental disturbance.

Vidal goes on to quote a Populus survey which found that '90% of respondents consider litter to be a massive issue'. By using percentage figures from a national organisation Vidal adds authority to his message. Such expert views, like Vidal's title, suggest that litter is bringing our country to the edge of calamity.

5 (AO3)

Possible answers

- Both Faraday and Vidal feel worried about how people have spoilt the landscape and they both seek action to resolve the problems they highlight.
- Faraday is worried about the way people have polluted the River Thames and Vidal seems concerned about flytipping and litter.
- Both writers are publishing their views in national newspapers to bring them to public attention.
- Vidal is addressing ordinary people in his article: some are careless but he is inviting them to change their ways. In contrast, Faraday hopes to address 'those who exercise power' in order to get the Thames cleaned.
- Vidal initially expresses his own observations of litter on the canal bank but later he supports the idea of a 'crisis' by introducing expert views.
- Both writers consider other ordinary people.
- Faraday weighs up his experience and wonders if others would share it. He writes, 'Having just returned from out of the country air, I was, perhaps, more affected by it than others'. This shows that he is able to consider perspectives other than his own.
- Vidal refers to the views of Chris, a retiree, to show that he considers other people's viewpoints.
- Both writers are horrified by what they see and they aim to share this sense of horror with their readers.
- Vidal uses listing to help people understand his feelings of horror. He lists many different items to show how much litter there is, including 'bags, butts and bottles'. Alliteration is used to draw attention to these items, making the list linger in the reader's mind. He suggests that many people contribute to the problem. He does this by referring to different groups like builders and 'kids', who all share the blame.
- Faraday shows his horror when he writes, 'The appearance and the smell of the water forced themselves at once on my attention'. This implies that the river has been so badly polluted that people have no choice but to breathe in the stale air. Here he uses personal experience to illustrate this idea.
- Each writer envisages worse problems in the future. Vidal quotes an expert who claims that we will soon see 'environmental degradation', whilst Faraday implies that the terrible state of the Thames will become the norm unless action is taken.

- At times Faraday's voice sounds like a preacher seeking to convert others. This is seen in the words, 'If we neglect this subject, we cannot expect to do so with impunity'. Here his choice of the word 'we' involves everybody in his cause.
- Vidal's own voice is not heard at the end of his piece. Readers are left to make up their own minds. Faraday speaks confidently in his own voice throughout but he shows us that he needs others, with direct responsibility for the Thames, to take action.

Sample student responses

Mid Level: Ideas and perspectives are compared in a clear and relevant way with reference to writers' methods. A clear understanding of the different ideas and perspectives in both texts is conveyed using relevant details. For example:

Faraday and Vidal both feel worried about people ruining the landscape. Vidal is primarily concerned about flytipping and litter whilst Faraday is worried about the way people have polluted the River Thames. They both seek to share their views and concerns by publishing them in newspapers in the hope that more people read them and think about them.

I think that Vidal's article is primarily designed to shock ordinary people into changing their ways, whilst Faraday's letter tries to persuade 'those who exercise power' to take action to clear up the Thames.

The headline of Vidal's piece tells readers that Britain is on the 'verge' of a litter crisis. This headline sums up the view he presents throughout the article. However, the word 'verge' shows that there is still time to turn back. The title of Faraday's letter uses the word 'filth' to show the dirty state of the Thames, which is his central concern.

At the start Vidal makes his own observations, but later on he brings in expert opinions to support his view that Britain is facing a litter crisis. This works and I am more likely to trust Government figures than one man. In contrast Faraday expresses his views in his own words.

These writers are revolted by what they see. Vidal wants to illustrate just how much rubbish is being thrown away so he lists many different items of rubbish to show how bad the problem is. By showing different kinds of litter he seems to say that, in his view, many people contribute to it.

In order to express his feelings of horror and revulsion, Faraday claims that the Thames could turn into a 'fermenting sewer' which sounds particularly disgusting as a sewer carries human waste. I think he does this to make readers imagine how unpleasant the water is in order to shock them since their ideal picture of this river might be very different.

In conclusion, the writers share similar views. They believe that the environment has been spoilt, and if action is not taken then there is no hope of a solution.

Higher Level: Ideas and perspectives are compared perceptively by analysing writers' methods and showing a detailed understanding of the different ideas and perspectives, using well-chosen details from both texts. For example:

Both Faraday and Vidal feel worried about the environments they are describing. They suggest that people have spoilt these places and that action needs to be taken. Each writer aims to share his views and experiences with the public by publishing them in the national press.

Faraday is primarily worried about the pollution of the River Thames. For example, he writes, 'The appearance and the smell of the water forced themselves at once on my attention'. He uses the word 'forced' to suggest that people must endure the pollution against their wills. Perhaps he does this to show his readers that many of them will be compelled to share his unpleasant experiences.

Vidal seems worried about the way that piles of litter impact on people's mental health. He quotes an expert called Richard McIlwain who believes 'people's sense of wellbeing will decline' as the rubbish increases. This could be designed to make his readers anxious.

Whilst Faraday expresses his views in his own voice, Vidal starts his article with personal observations and then supports these with authoritative sources. By doing this, Vidal is able to support his viewpoint with quantitative data such as the fact that one year the Highways Agency dealt with '852,000 flytipping incidents in England and Wales'. He draws on sources in order to convince readers that he is right when he suggests that people's behaviour is leading to a litter 'crisis'.

The two men both try to consider how other people would view the problems they describe. Faraday aims to weigh up his experiences in order to consider whether they are personal or universal. For example, when he is criticising the poor air quality, he acknowledges that his attitude may be coloured by his recent trip to the country where the air was presumably very fresh. He states, 'Having just returned from out of the country air, I was, perhaps, more affected by it than others.'

Vidal also considers other people's views when he quotes a retiree called Chris. Chris represents the 'person on the street' and shows that other ordinary people share Vidal's concerns. Vidal states that Chris finds the litter 'offensive, depressing and incomprehensible'. These words suggest that the litter has upset Chris and that therefore it may upset others.

Faraday implies that he is simply telling the truth and assures readers that 'there is nothing figurative in the words I have employed, or any approach to exaggeration'. However, when he implies that 'London ought not to be allowed to become a fermenting sewer', the words 'fermenting sewer' may seem exaggerated and emotive since a sewer carries waste such as faeces and 'fermenting' means brewing up, which reminds us of the 'bad smell' he referred to earlier. These words seem designed to make the future seem bleak.

While Vidal draws on expert opinions, Faraday expresses his own views strongly throughout his letter and at times his tone resembles that of a preacher seeking to convert the ignorant. For example, 'If we neglect this subject, we cannot expect to do so with impunity'. His choice of the word 'we' deliberately implicates everybody in his cause. He sounds like a preacher because he suggests that those who don't act may be punished (presumably by the deterioration of the Thames).

Both men therefore consider the plight of ordinary people and the destruction of the environment. Their ultimate aim is to encourage others to take action.

Turn over for Question 6 answers

Paper 2: Section B

 (AO5) (AO6)

Sample student responses

Lower Level: Sometimes matched to purpose and audience. There is an attempt to use a varied vocabulary and some linguistic devices. At times the writing is clear and contains linked, relevant ideas with occasional variety in sentence structures. Some of the grammar and spelling is correct. For example:

> This greeting is too informal; 'Ladies and Gentlemen' would be appropriate

> Some attempt to establish structure

Hello Council,

I am here to tell you my ideas about sorting out our town so that it looks better.

Firstly, you need to sort out the piles of rubbish around the edges of the sports ground. I go there every week and I've seen all kinds of stuff dumped there. For a start, there are two shopping trollies, a fridge and a dirty, torn mattress. My first idea is to get a van up there and ask the football club to help you clear away all these items. I am in one of the teams and I could ask my friends to help you out.

> Avoid using the word 'stuff'– 'items' would be a better word

The second issue is that the beach looks like a tip. No body picks up their fish and chip wrappers and there are empty cans floating in the sea. Could you get a team of people down there to pick litter up each night? If you put up out an advert, I am sure some people would volunteer. It would be great if the beach looked nice again and it would bring in more visitors.

> 'Nobody' is one word, not two

> The word 'nice' is simplistic and best avoided; 'attractive' could be used instead

Those new-style toilets in the middle of town are another issue [I mean the new ones that look at bit like the Tardis]. They have been ruined already because all the doors have been damaged and sprayed with swear words.

I have another point about the same toilets. I think they need checking out because last week my Gran went into one and got stuck in there. We couldn't get her out so we kicked the doors [which made them look even worse]. Gran was in there for over half an hour crying so all sorts of people tried to get her out and there woz a lot more damage to the door.

> No attempt at structure, simply adds on another point

> Incorrect spelling of 'was'

I think that you need to get the locking systems checked out so nobody else needs to kick there way in or out. Once this locking system is sorted, then repair the doors and remove the graffiti at the same time. Maybe whoever wrote the rude graffiti was cross because they couldn't get into a loo or out of it.

> This is the wrong 'there'; it should be 'their'

So, I suggest you clear the sports ground, pick up litter on the beach and check and repair the toilet doors. I reckon these three things will make a big difference as people visit all these places often.

Do you have any questions?

> This paragraph attempts to sum up the main points in conclusion

> 'I reckon' is too informal; 'I suggest' would be better

Mid Level: Generally well matched to purpose and audience. The vocabulary is chosen for effect and includes some sophisticated word choices, using linguistic devices successfully. The writing is engaging and it contains a range of clear, connected ideas. A variety of sentence forms are used for effect. Grammar, punctuation and spelling (including the spelling of complex words) are all good. For example:

> *Ladies and Gentlemen,*
>
> *I have come to speak to you today about various problems in our local environment and I have also got some suggestions about how you can deal with them.*
>
> *The first problem I have noticed is graffiti. This has got worse over the last few years. The pictures on the walls outside the town hall are particularly offensive. If you don't control this problem soon, it is going to get worse and I think that teenagers are probably responsible. My solution is to provide a huge graffiti wall in a less public area and to invite creative teenagers to display their work there. You could even bring in an art instructor to give them ideas and show them how to use spray paints.*
>
> *The second problem is dog mess. My mother gets furious when I tread it into the hall carpet on the bottom of my shoes but I can't help it. There is so much of it on the pavements that it is almost impossible not to step in something. This problem is really disgusting and you must find a way to sort it out. Why don't you try doubling the number of dog bins in the town because it seems that every second person has a dog? I realise this will cost lots of money but if there is less mess then there will be less tension between those who have dogs and those who don't.*
>
> *Thirdly, could you fence off a few of the green areas? While they open directly onto the road, most parents are afraid to let their younger children play there. Fences would also make them look neater. Perhaps you could plant some pretty flowers around the edges. We could even enter Britain in Bloom – wouldn't that be great?*
>
> *Finally, there are all sorts of nasty bits of litter floating in the lake in the park. The other day I saw a swan with a plastic bag tangled in its feet. Luckily, it managed to shake it off but it could happen again. Somebody needs to take a boat out onto the lake and clear the mess up. Perhaps you could also put up a notice to remind people that rubbish can be harmful to water birds. I would be happy to go out in a boat with a couple of my friends and fish out the litter.*
>
> *I know that most of the problems have been caused by thoughtless people, and that you have to clear up after them, but these changes could really improve the environment.*
>
> *I am happy to help and I would certainly like to try out the new graffiti wall, if you get one. I believe that this city can be pretty and clean again. Let's work together to make it happen.*

Annotations:

- This opening is matched to the purpose of the task
- The use of 'The first problem' in the previous paragraph and 'The second problem' here helps to provide a clear structure for this piece
- Once again the argument is clearly indicated
- Informal/colloquial; it would be better to say 'unpleasant'
- The word 'pretty' is used again here; it would be better to use more sophisticated vocabulary
- By presenting a problem and then a solution, the student shows that he or she is clearly answering the question
- Use of anecdote
- Aim for a more formal alternative, e.g. 'attractive'
- Uses a personal anecdote
- Good call to action at the end; more sophisticated vocabulary could be used throughout

Higher Level: This answer is confidently matched to purpose and audience; vocabulary is extensive and ambitious and writing is compelling and fluently linked, using a full range of sentence forms for effect. Grammar, punctuation and spelling (including the spelling of ambitious vocabulary) are all excellent. For example:

A confident opening which is matched to the purpose of the task →

Thank you for inviting me to speak to the council today. *As you are aware, I am here to propose a number of measures that could significantly improve our environment.*

At present we are sinking under a sea of litter. Drinks cans clatter and rattle *along our pavements while cardboard cups drift lazily down rivers. The other day I even saw two crisp packets flying towards me like empty enemy parachutes.*

← Use of assonance

Effective use of a simile →

We are also experiencing an unprecedented *level of flytipping.* Sneaky *residents are creeping about after dark to furtively abandon unwanted furniture and fixings on the river banks and in green areas. Among these items lurk their more sinister companions: abandoned bags liners full of stinking chicken carcases and soiled nappies. Such gruesome items have attracted rats! These creatures are becoming a nationwide problem.* Are you aware that the rat population in Britain is over sixty million?

← Sophisticated word choice

'Sneaky' is a little too informal →

← Uses appropriate supporting evidence and a direct question

A powerful image is used to illustrate the state of the paper bank →

I appreciate that you are a proactive council and applaud your recent installation of recycling bins in all three major carparks. However, the last time I walked through Vernon Street carpark, I noticed the great mouth of a paper bank straining to contain its oozing load, as if it had never been emptied.

Ladies and Gentlemen, while I believe that you are doing your utmost to shoulder these responsibilities, you are a tiny troop struggling to do the work of a battalion. Therefore I suggest that we work together to enlist a team of willing volunteers. Any rat-infested bin bags should be removed by specialist disposal teams, but the unwanted furniture items could be collected by adult volunteers. Perhaps you could paint, repair and reuse *them?*

← Uses a pattern of three

Use of anecdote →

I also recommend that you double the number of collections from local recycling bins to prevent them from becoming an eyesore. Then you could move forwards by suggesting even more recycling opportunities. In year seven, I visited the Southwark Discovery Centre on a Geography trip. During this outing I learned about the vast array of items that can be repaired, recycled or renewed. *Since then I have actively campaigned for posters and information leaflets in my school.*

I hope my speech has provided you with some practical, cost-effective solutions to improve our environment. If you don't want to see our town engulfed in litter or crawling with rats, then follow my suggestions. Thank you for listening to my suggestions so attentively. Let's work together to make things better.

← Ends with an appropriate call to action

PART THREE: YORK NOTES PRACTICE TEST TWO

Paper 1: Reading and writing imaginative/creative texts

Instructions

- Time allowed: 1 hour 45 minutes*
- The text material is printed within this practice paper. Please refer to this in your answers.
- Answer **all** questions.
- Answer the questions in the space provided, continuing onto a separate sheet if needed.
- Do all rough work in a notebook or on separate sheets of paper.
- You should **not** use a dictionary.

Information for candidates

- There are two sections: **Section A** (Reading) and **Section B** (Writing).
- Section A (Reading): 40 marks
- Section B (Writing): 40 marks
- The number of marks is given in brackets at the end of each question.

Advice

- Read each question carefully before you start to answer it.
- Check your answers if you have time at the end.

Some exam boards/organisations allow 2 hours for this paper.

Text A

This extract is taken from a Sherlock Holmes crime novel called The Hound of the Baskervilles *by Sir Arthur Conan Doyle. This book was first published in serial form in 1901–2. In this extract Holmes and Watson hear a terrible sound on the moors.*

Holmes had sprung to his feet, and I saw his dark, athletic outline at the door of the hut, his shoulders stooping, his head thrust forward, his face peering into the darkness.

'Hush!' he whispered. 'Hush!'

5 The cry had been loud on account of its vehemence, but it had pealed out from somewhere far off on the shadowy plain. Now it burst upon our ears, nearer, louder, more urgent than before.

'Where is it?' Holmes whispered; and I knew from the thrill of his voice that he, the man of iron, was shaken to the soul. 'Where is it, Watson?'

'There, I think.' I pointed into the darkness.

10 'No, there!'

Again the agonized cry swept through the silent night, louder and much nearer than ever. And a new sound mingled with it, a deep, muttered rumble, musical and yet menacing, rising and falling like the low, constant murmur of the sea.

'The hound!' cried Holmes. 'Come, Watson, come! Great heavens, if we are too late!'

15 He had started running swiftly over the moor, and I had followed at his heels. But now from somewhere among the broken ground immediately in front of us there came one last despairing yell, and then a dull, heavy thud. We halted and listened. Not another sound broke the heavy silence of the windless night.

I saw Holmes put his hand to his forehead like a man distracted.[1] He stamped his feet upon
20 the ground.

'He has beaten us, Watson. We are too late.'

'No, no, surely not!'

'Fool that I was to hold my hand.[2] And you, Watson, see what comes of abandoning your charge! But, by Heaven, if the worst has happened we'll avenge him!'

25 Blindly we ran through the gloom, blundering against boulders, forcing our way through gorse bushes, panting up hills and rushing down slopes, heading always in the direction whence those dreadful sounds had come. At every rise Holmes looked eagerly round him, but the shadows were thick upon the moor, and nothing moved upon its dreary face.

'Can you see anything?'

30 'Nothing.'

'But, hark, what is that?'

A low moan had fallen upon our ears. There it was again upon our left! On that side a ridge of rocks ended in a sheer cliff which overlooked a stone-strewn slope. On its jagged face was spread-eagled some dark, irregular object. As we ran towards it the vague outline

35 hardened into a definite shape. It was a prostrate man face downward upon the ground, the head doubled under him at a horrible angle, the shoulders rounded and the body hunched together as if in the act of throwing a somersault. So grotesque was the attitude that I could not for the instant realize that that moan had been the passing of his soul. Not a whisper, not a rustle, rose now from the dark figure over which we stooped. Holmes laid

40 his hand upon him and held it up again, with an exclamation of horror. The gleam of the match which he struck shone upon his clotted fingers and upon the ghastly pool which widened slowly from the crushed skull of the victim. And it shone upon something else which turned our hearts sick and faint within us – the body of Sir Henry Baskerville!

There was no chance of either of us forgetting that peculiar ruddy tweed suit – the very one

45 which he had worn on the first morning that we had seen him in Baker Street. We caught the one clear glimpse of it, and then the match flickered and went out, even as the hope had gone out of our souls. Holmes groaned, and his face glimmered white through the darkness.

'The brute! the brute!' I cried with clenched hands. 'Oh Holmes, I shall never forgive myself for having left him to his fate.'

Glossary

distracted[1] – mentally confused or deeply troubled by grief and anxiety.
hold my hand[2] – wait without taking action.

Turn over for Section A

Section A: Reading

Answer **all** questions in this section.
You are advised to spend about half the exam time on this section.

❶ Read again the first part of the text, **lines 1 to 13**.

List **four** things from this part of the text about the sound the two men hear.

(4 marks)

1 _____

_____

2 _____

_____

3 _____

_____

4 _____

_____

❷ Look in detail at this extract from **lines 14 to 28** of the text:

'The hound!' cried Holmes. 'Come, Watson, come! Great heavens, if we are too late!'

He had started running swiftly over the moor, and I had followed at his heels. But now from somewhere among the broken ground immediately in front of us there came one last despairing yell, and then a dull, heavy thud. We halted and listened. Not another sound broke the heavy silence of the windless night.

I saw Holmes put his hand to his forehead like a man distracted. He stamped his feet upon the ground.

'He has beaten us, Watson. We are too late.'

'No, no, surely not!'

'Fool that I was to hold my hand. And you, Watson, see what comes of abandoning your charge! But, by Heaven, if the worst has happened we'll avenge him!'

Blindly we ran through the gloom, blundering against boulders, forcing our way through gorse bushes, panting up hills and rushing down slopes, heading always in the direction whence those dreadful sounds had come. At every rise Holmes looked eagerly round him, but the shadows were thick upon the moor, and nothing moved upon its dreary face.

How does the writer use language here to convey Holmes's desperation?

You could comment on the writer's choice of:

- words and phrases
- language features and techniques
- sentence forms.

(8 marks)

_____

_____

_____

_____

_____

_____

_____

_____

_____

_____

_____

_____

_____

_____

_____

_____

_____

_____

_____

_____

_____

_____

3 You now need to think about the **whole** of the text.

This text is taken from a chapter near the end of the novel *The Hound of the Baskervilles*.

How has the writer structured the text to interest you as a reader?

You could write about:

- what the writer focuses your attention on at the beginning of the text
- how and why the writer changes this focus as the text develops
- any other structural features that interest you.

(8 marks)

_____

_____

_____

_____

_____

_____

_____

_____

_____

_____

_____

_____

_____

_____

_____

_____

_____

_____

_____

_____

_____

_____

_____

_____

4 Now look at the last part of the text, **from line 29 to the end.**

A student, having read this section of the text, said: 'The writer makes the moment when Holmes and Watson find the body very dramatic. I can feel the tension rising as I read it'.

To what extent do you agree?

In your response, you could:

● write about your own impressions of the discovery of the body
● evaluate how the writer has created these impressions
● support your opinions with references to the text.

(20 marks)

Section B: Writing

You are advised to spend about half the exam time on this section.
Write in full sentences.
You are reminded of the need to plan your answer.
You should leave enough time to check your work at the end.

5 Write a description suggested by this picture:

(24 marks for content and organisation
16 marks for technical accuracy)

(40 marks)

_____

_____

_____

_____

_____

_____

_____

END OF QUESTIONS

Paper 2: Reading and writing non-fiction texts

Instructions

- Time allowed: 1 hour 45 minutes*
- The text material is printed within this practice paper. Please refer to this in your answers.
- Answer **all** questions.
- Answer the questions in the space provided, continuing onto a separate sheet if needed.
- Do all rough work in a notebook or on separate sheets of paper.
- You should **not** use a dictionary.

Information for candidates

- There are two sections: **Section A** (Reading) and **Section B** (Writing).
- Section A (Reading): 40 marks
- Section B (Writing): 40 marks
- The number of marks is given in brackets at the end of each question.

Advice

- Read each question carefully before you start to answer it.
- Check your answers if you have time at the end.

Some exam boards/organisations allow 2 hours for this paper.

Text A

This text is an extract from an article written for The Guardian *by a father contemplating the long school summer holidays.*

Why working parents like me dread the summer holidays

The Guardian, Friday 22 July 2016 by Andy Dawson (theguardian.com)

Before it appears that I'm some kind of villainous dad, I need to establish that ever since they came into my life, my overriding purpose in life has been to be a diligent, devoted parent to my two children [...]

5   But each year when the summer holidays loom I transform into a twitchy, cranky mess, breaking out in cold sweats and clawing at my own skin as I fret about what's to come once they've been turfed through the school gate for the last time.

If you're a working parent of a school-age child, you know exactly what I'm talking about. If you haven't been dreading the onset of the summer break and the impossible work/ parenting juggle that comes with it, you're a liar.

10   On one hand I'm incredibly lucky that, as a freelance writer, I get to work from home and am usually unimpeded by obstacles such as fixed working hours or a remote workplace (although the thought of such sanctuary has its appeal).

Having said that, I also have to write 30,000 words of a book between now and the end of August, which means that it's going to get really, really tense around here when the
15   children's mum is occupied with her proper job. In fact, I had to get out of bed at 5am just to find the time to write this piece, but that's OK.

We're not short of things to do – we live a couple of miles from the north-east coast and a short car ride away from the majestic Northumberland countryside, so day trips are well catered for. Plus there's the new-found wonders of Pokémon Go – less than a week
20   into that craze and we're all sporting [...] tans from extended adventures in the sunshine.

But the book deadline means I can't afford to take a sustained period off work, which leaves us with those days when we're all rattling around the house, getting right on each other's wick.

25   As such, a domestic state of emergency kicks into operation. The house as we know it ceases to exist. Any kind of structure or order flies out of the window, with chores abandoned and the ironing pile relocated to a hidden bubble of space behind the settee so we can all pretend it isn't there.

30   Bits of Lego, random action figures and hundreds of collector cards are strewn all over the
floor, with the living room now resembling a toy shop that has been ransacked in a riot.

Try as I might to get some work done, it's as laborious as pushing a golf ball up a custard
mountain with the tip of my nose. The kids seem to have developed some sort of innate,
unspoken tag team system. The moment I sit down after finishing a 20-minute football
match in the garden with the boy one, the girl one appears and wants to know if she can
35   have some strawberries or whether I know why the printer has stopped working.

You know you're broken when you find yourself on eBay, researching the cost of those
paper boiler suits that decorators and lab technicians wear. We'll all look daft, but it'll cut
right down on laundry.

There's always the option of farming them out (in the nicest possible way, obviously) to
40   someone else, but the cost is too great, be it financially (childcare fees are exorbitant) or
emotionally (their grandparents are now shattered husks, wrecked from more than a
decade of ad hoc babysitting).

It's not just the days – the summer holidays blight your evenings too. Extensions to regular
bedtimes mean that the younglings are mooching about the house well after 11pm.
45   Thinking of catching up on the last series of Game of Thrones at the end of a hard day's
life-juggling? Better get your finger poised over the remote in case they wander in from
their respective leisure spaces to submit some kind of random cheese enquiry or ask if
you can evict a spider from the bathroom.

The whole thing is a lot like regular parenting, only filtered through a psychedelic
50   kaleidoscope and played out at three times its usual speed. You quickly realise how much
of the strain of child-rearing is carried by the education system, and you vow never to
make one of those snide remarks about teachers knocking off at half three each day and
spending most of their lives on holiday.

Text B

This text is taken from a letter written by George Gissing, an English novelist who lived from 1857–1903. His letter describes a national bank holiday in 1882.

It is Bank Holiday to-day, and the streets are overcrowded with swarms of people. Never is so clearly to be seen the vulgarity of the people as at these holiday times. Their notion of a holiday is to rush in crowds to some sweltering place, such as the Crystal Palace,[1] and there sit and drink and quarrel themselves into stupidity. Miserable children are lugged

5   about, yelling at the top of their voices, and are beaten because they yell. Troops of hideous creatures drive wildly about the town in gigs,[2] donkey-carts, cabbage-carts, dirt-carts, and think it enjoyment. The pleasure of peace and quietness, of rest for body and mind, is not understood. Thousands are tempted by cheap trips to go off for the day to the seaside, and succeed in wearying themselves to death, for the sake of eating a greasy

10   meal in a 10 Margate Coffee-shop, and getting five minutes' glimpse of the sea through eyes blinded with dirt and perspiration. Places like Hampstead Heath and the various parks and commons are packed with screeching drunkards, one general mass of dust and heat and rage and exhaustion. Yet this is the best kind of holiday the people are capable of.

It is utterly absurd, this idea of setting aside single days for great public holidays. It will

15   never do anything but harm. What we want is a general shortening of the working hours all year round, so that, for instance, all labour would be over at 4 o'clock in the afternoon. Then the idea of hours of leisure would become familiar to the people and they would learn to make some sensible use of them. Of course this is impossible so long as we work for working's sake. All the world's work – all that is really necessary for the health and

20   comfort and even luxury of mankind – could be performed in three or four hours of each day. There is so much labour just because there is so much money-grubbing. Every man has to fight for a living with his neighbour, and the grocer who keeps his shop open till half an hour after midnight has an advantage over him who closes at twelve. Work in itself is *not an end; only a means;* but we nowadays make it an end, and three-fourths of the

25   world cannot understand anything else.

Glossary

Crystal Palace[1] – a large, glass building in London which was often used for shows, concerts and exhibitions.

gigs[2] – a gig is a two-wheeled carriage pulled by a horse.

Section A: Reading

Answer **all** questions in this section.
You are advised to spend about half the exam time on this section.

1 Read again the first part of **Text A, lines 1 to 16**.

Choose **four** statements below which are TRUE.

- Tick the boxes of the ones that you think are true.
- Choose a maximum of four statements.

(4 marks)

A Andy Dawson claims to be devoted to his children. ☐

B Andy Dawson dreads the end of term. ☐

C As a writer, Andy Dawson faces fewer work complications than some other parents. ☐

D Andy Dawson has never wanted to work in a remote location. ☐

E Andy Dawson believes other parents share his feelings about school holidays. ☐

F Andy Dawson is not concerned about his approaching deadline. ☐

G The children's mother also works from home. ☐

H Andy Dawson always gets up at 5am to work. ☐

2 You need to refer to **Text A** and **Text B** for this question:

Use details from **both** texts. Write a summary of the differences between the problems that these writers associate with holidays.

(8 marks)

_____

_____

_____

_____

_____

_____

_____

_____

_____

_____

_____

_____

_____

_____

_____

_____

_____

_____

_____

_____

_____

_____

_____

_____

_____

_____

❸ You now need to refer **only** to **Text B**, the letter by Gissing.

How does Gissing use language to suggest that bank holidays make people unhappy?

(12 marks)

4 For this question, you need to refer to the **whole of Text A** together with **Text B**.

Compare how the two writers convey their feelings about holidays.

In your answer, you could:

- compare their different feelings
- compare the methods they use to convey their feelings
- support your ideas with references to both texts.

(16 marks)

_____

_____

_____

_____

_____

_____

_____

_____

_____

_____

_____

_____

_____

_____

_____

_____

_____

_____

_____

_____

_____

_____

Section B: Writing

You are advised to spend about half the exam time on this section.
Write in full sentences.
You are reminded of the need to plan your answer.
You should leave enough time to check your work at the end.

5 'School summer holidays are too long. Most students get bored as the weeks drag on and they forget much of what they have learned. Students should spend more time at school.'

Write an article for a broadsheet newspaper in which you explain your point of view on this statement.

(24 marks for content and organisation
16 marks for technical accuracy)

(40 marks)

_____

_____

_____

_____

_____

_____

_____

_____

_____

_____

_____

_____

_____

_____

_____

_____

_____

_____

_____

_____

75

END OF QUESTIONS

Answers and sample responses

Paper 1: Section A

❶ (AO1)

Any four or more answers from the following:

- It was loud.
- It 'pealed out from somewhere far off'.
- It became louder and more urgent.
- It was vehement.
- It was an 'agonized cry' that 'swept through the silent night'.
- A 'new sound mingled with it, a deep, muttered rumble'.
- It was 'musical and yet menacing, rising and falling like the low, constant murmur of the sea'.

❷ (AO2)

Possible answers

- Exclamation marks are used to convey a sense of urgency in the line '"The hound!" cried Holmes'. "Come, Watson, come! Great heavens, if we are too late!"'
- There are three of these exclamation marks so the writer is using a pattern of three to highlight the strength of Holmes's emotions.
- These same sentences are short and sharp to suggest that Holmes is in a rush and can't waste words.
- The combination of the verb 'running' with the adverb 'swiftly' suggests fast movement.
- A simile is used in 'I saw Holmes put his hand to his forehead like a man distracted'. Here 'distracted' means agitated or deeply troubled, suggesting that Holmes could not behave in a logical manner.
- Holmes says, 'Fool that I was to hold my hand. And you, Watson, see what comes of abandoning your charge!' By using the noun 'fool' he is being self-critical. He follows this up by blaming Watson for leaving Sir Henry. This comment is marked by an exclamation mark to show strong emotion.
- The complex sentence which begins with the words 'Blindly we ran through the gloom, blundering against boulders' uses alliteration since 'blindly', 'blundering' and 'boulders' all begin with 'b'. This alliteration draws attention to the men's stumbling movements and the obstacles in their path.
- The verb 'blundering' begins a cumulative list of verbs ('panting', 'rushing' and 'heading'), all suggesting ongoing action.
- This sentence is also broken up by commas which may represent Holmes's shortness of breath. This idea is reinforced by the writer's use of the verb 'panting'.
- The adverb 'blindly' suggests that Holmes was not thinking about what he was doing.
- The verb 'blundering' implies carelessness.
- The verb 'rushing' shows that he was moving very quickly.
- The words 'forcing our way through gorse bushes' imply that the route was painful because gorse bushes have thorns on them and a rational person would avoid the pain of being scratched.
- The writer's use of the adverb 'eagerly' could suggest impatience or anxiety.

Sample student responses

Mid Level: A clear understanding of language, with relevant details, effects explained and accurate terminology. For example:

The writer says Holmes 'had started running swiftly over the moor'. The adverb 'swiftly' emphasises that Holmes is moving very fast and this speed shows his desperation. When we are told that he is 'like a man distracted' it has the effect of making us realise that Holmes felt very upset. Here the writer uses a simile which gives us a clear picture of Holmes being 'distracted' which means troubled. We can also tell that Holmes is rushing because of the alliteration used in 'Blindly we ran through the gloom, blundering against boulders, forcing our way through gorse bushes, panting up hills and rushing down slopes'. The verbs here create a lot of movement while the alliteration draws attention to his route, helping us to imagine a scene where Holmes is rushing across the moors in desperation.

Higher Level: Detailed and perceptive understanding of language with very well-chosen details, analysis of the effects of the writer's choices and sophisticated use of terminology. For example:

The opening of this extract uses a series of short, sharp, commanding sentences punctuated by exclamation marks to convey Holmes's desperation. In the same lines, the writer employs the pattern of three to highlight the extremity of Holmes's feelings: '"The hound!" cried Holmes. "Come, Watson, come! Great heavens, if we are too late!"'

Holmes indicates desperation when he flings out accusations: 'Fool that I was to hold my hand' and 'Watson, see what comes of abandoning your charge!' By using the noun 'fool' to describe himself Holmes is being highly self-critical and he quickly follows this up by also blaming Watson. In addition, the simile 'Holmes put his hand to his forehead like a man distracted' implies that Holmes is deeply troubled and has abandoned his usual calm reasoning abilities.

The dramatic use of a complex alliterative sentence beginning 'Blindly we ran through the gloom, blundering against boulders' reflects a sense of rushing momentum where the verb 'blundering' begins a list of 'ing' verbs ('panting', 'rushing' and 'heading'), with a cumulative effect suggesting continuous ongoing action. This sentence is also broken up by commas which might represent Holmes's shortness of breath as he rushes forwards. Finally, the adverb 'eagerly' suggests Holmes's anxiety and impatience.

❸ (AO2)

Possible answers

- The text is structured so that it propels readers quickly through the action.
- The piece begins with Holmes jumping to his feet, suggesting that something dramatic is happening.
- The reader is immediately drawn into the urgency of the situation by sharp snatches of dialogue.
- This dialogue is intermingled with descriptions of the noise in order to draw the reader's attention back to the strange sound and make them want to find out what it is.
- Around the middle of the extract, the focus shifts when Holmes starts running, with Watson following quickly behind him.
- The reader is rushed along, accompanying the two men as they dash 'blindly' across the moors.
- Like the men, the text itself is heading towards the place where the strange sound seems to be coming from.
- The noise is presented as getting closer and closer until it is located on the men's left.
- As Holmes and Watson approach the cliff, the focus of the text gradually narrows towards the body.
- Conan Doyle brings his readers increasingly closer to this dead body, which changes from a 'vague outline' to a 'definite shape'. Then the writer focuses in even more to reveal 'the body of Sir Henry Baskerville'.
- Further closely observed details about the body are provided when the reader is told that it is dressed in a distinctive 'tweed suit'.
- At the end of this episode the writer moves his focus away from the body and back to Holmes's and Watson's horrified reactions to it.

Sample student responses

Mid Level: A clear understanding of structural features with a range of relevant examples referred to using accurate terminology. For example:

The writer focuses the reader's attention on Holmes jumping up at the beginning of this episode. This shows us that this text is about something dramatic. Then he reveals what has caught Holmes's attention by describing the noise when he writes 'The cry had been loud'. This involves readers in the action because they wonder what the sound is.

The writer then shifts the focus away from the noise, describing the two men running towards it. Holmes runs with Watson 'at his heels'. This running section continues at a rapid pace as the writer draws attention to the men 'forcing our way through gorse bushes, panting up hills and rushing down slopes'. Throughout this part the reader feels like he or she is with the men on their chase.

Next the body is revealed at a distance. At first it seems unclear but gradually the writer moves his focus closer and closer until it is identified. Holmes and Watson become distressed when they realise the dead man is Sir Henry so the writer changes focus by shifting attention to their emotions rather than the dead body.

Higher Level: Detailed and perceptive understanding of structural features with a very well-chosen range of examples and analysis of the effects of these features using sophisticated terminology. For example:

The text, which is about a desperate rush to prevent murder, is structured so that the reader feels he/she is being propelled quickly through it: from the opening when Holmes jumps to his feet, to the men's chase across the moors and then finally to the dreadful moment when the body is discovered and identified. Readers are immediately drawn into the urgency of the situation by snatches of dialogue such as 'No, there!' and by descriptions of a strange cry.

Around the middle of the extract, the focus shifts to the chase as Holmes starts 'running swiftly' over the moor with Watson 'at his heels'. The reader is then rushed along, accompanying these men through a bleak terrain of 'boulders' and 'gorse bushes'. Like them, the text is 'heading always in the direction whence those dreadful sounds had come'. However, as they approach the cliff, the writer's focus narrows dramatically as it moves closer and closer to the dead body, which is conveyed first as a 'vague outline' and then as a 'definite shape' and finally as 'the body of Sir Henry Baskerville' dressed in his distinctive 'tweed suit'. Finally, the writer shifts attention away from the victim and back to Holmes and Watson as their horrified reactions to their discovery are revealed.

(AO4)

Possible answers

- The question 'But, hark, what is that?' makes us want to read on to discover what has been heard.
- A 'low moan' sounds as if somebody is suffering or in pain.
- The words 'There it was again upon our left!' give us the impression that the men are moving continually closer to the sound. The exclamation mark suggests desperation and urgency.
- The description of the cliff face as 'sheer' and 'jagged' implies that the setting was sinister and dangerous.
- The men 'ran' towards the sound, which suggests they were in a desperate hurry.
- The writer builds tension by revealing the body slowly. Conan Doyle encourages readers to imagine a 'vague outline' changing to become a 'definite shape'.
- The way that the writer has positioned the body 'face downward' delays its identification and builds the tension further.
- The line 'Not a whisper, not a rustle, rose now from the dark figure over which we stooped' suggests a tense pause in the action which contrasts with the earlier rush.
- The descriptions of the body ('horrible angle', 'crushed skull' and 'body hunched') are extremely vivid and effective at painting a clear, if brutal, picture.
- The fact that the body can only be seen by the 'gleam of' a match suggests that each part is revealed faintly through flickering light.
- They had to light a match because it was dark, which makes the scene seem more eerie.
- Night-time seems to be a fitting setting for a murder and Gothic fiction often included sinister events set against a backdrop of darkness.
- Once the body is identified as Sir Henry Baskerville, we realise that Holmes and Watson know him. This makes the death seem more shocking.
- When the match goes out it effectively symbolises the death of hope.
- The men seem to have failed in their mission so the chase was for nothing. Now they can only experience horror and despair.
- The word 'groaned' conveys Holmes's despair and indicates (like the earlier moan) how sound is being used to enhance the drama of the piece.
- The statement 'The brute! the brute!' implies that the murderer was particularly cruel.

Sample student responses

Mid Level: A clear and relevant evaluation, which uses a range of textual details to evaluate the effect(s) on the reader. This answer shows a clear understanding of the writer's methods and a relevant response to the statement in the question. For example:

I agree that this passage is full of tension and drama. In fact, the subject matter is dramatic since the writer is describing two men approaching a dead body and hearing strange sounds in the middle of the night.

Holmes and Watson hear a 'low moan' which intrigues the reader and builds up tension as we seek to discover the cause of such a dreadful noise. Then, when the men approach the body, the writer reveals its identity slowly so that a 'vague outline' gradually turns out to be a person the men actually know, Sir Henry Baskerville. To add to the drama, the writer describes the body as being 'horrific' and 'grotesque', which conveys the image of something terrible. Readers also learn that the corpse has a cracked skull, which implies that a very cruel crime has been committed.

When a match goes out and the two men are left in darkness we are told that 'the hope had gone'. This breaks the tension that was created during the chase and the discovery of the body because there is nothing more that Holmes and Watson can do to help the victim. However, readers are reminded of the dramatic events that have taken place when the two men express their feelings and the murderer is called a 'brute' twice, which makes him sound very unpleasant.

Higher Level: Shows perceptive and detailed evaluation using a very well-chosen range of textual details to evaluate the effect(s) on the reader. This answer shows perceptive understanding of the writer's methods and develops a convincing and critical response to the statement in the question. For example:

I do agree that this episode is both tense and dramatic since it portrays the discovery of a disfigured body and the gradual and dreadful revelation of its identity. This drama begins when Holmes asks, 'hark, what is that?' Conan Doyle then goes on to define the noise as a 'low moan' (a sound normally associated with pain or suffering), creating the impression that Holmes and Watson are closing in on something sinister. From this moment, the reader shares the men's feelings of dread and anticipation as they rush towards the place where the moan emanated from. The writer's choice of setting, a 'sheer cliff' with a 'jagged face', enhances the drama because a 'sheer cliff' seems perilous and 'jagged' implies something sharp.

Conan Doyle also builds dramatic tension by slowly revealing a 'dark irregular object'. He then further delays the moment of revelation as 'the vague outline hardened into a definite shape', implying that the two men are moving closer and closer to the corpse.

The strange positioning of the body develops the tension further by obscuring its identity for even longer because it is 'prostrate' and 'face downward upon the ground'. Conan Doyle deliberately arranges the victim with 'the head doubled under him at a horrible angle', leaving his readers waiting to discover who it is.

Time seems to stand still when the narrator states, 'Not a whisper, not a rustle, rose now from the dark figure over which we stooped'. This moment of drama cleverly contrasts the previous chase with stillness and silence. Furthermore, the vivid references to a 'ghastly pool' and 'crushed skull' paint a powerful picture, implying that the victim's death was inflicted brutally and increasing the horror of the situation.

In my view, the most dramatic moment in this extract is when Holmes and Watson finally identify the body and recognise the distinctive 'tweed suit' of Sir Henry Baskerville. It is implied that they knew Sir Henry from a previous episode at 'Baker Street'. Therefore, it seems likely that they feel shocked and traumatised.

When 'the match flickered and went out' the reader realises that all hope is lost. Once this happens, I believe that the urgency and drama dissipate since all Holmes's and Watson's frantic efforts have, tragically, proved futile.

Turn over for Question 5 answers

Paper 1: Section B

 (AO5) (AO6)

Sample student responses

Lower Level: Sometimes matched to purpose and audience. There is an attempt to use a varied vocabulary and some linguistic devices. At times the writing is clear and contains linked, relevant ideas with occasional variety in sentence structures. Some of the grammar and spelling is correct. For example:

> Some use of linguistic devices (simile); the image could be more imaginative

A teenage girl is running through the woods. The grass is thin but green. It waves in the wind. Her path looks like a river between two lines of trees. The sharp branches are as dangerous as daggers*.*

> The student has changed tense here; he/she was writing in the present tense but has now changed to the past tense, indicated by the 'ed' ending

The girl is nearly at the top of the hill. As she sprinted *along, with the trees lining her way, she starts getting hot because of her thick black coat. She has rolled up her jeans to stop them catching in her trainers and she is a good runner so she doesn't get out of breath even after her long climb.*

> The sentence starting 'Down through the trees' is not correct as it should be part of the sentence before

A storm has broken off lots of the branches. She has to jump over a few that have fallen on the path. But the weather seems sunny now and light shines. Down through the trees *making her feel happy. It is the perfect day to be out in the countryside and she is keen to find out what* beautiful *scenes she might find around the next corner.*

> Adjective choices could be more interesting

Mid Level: Generally well matched to purpose and audience. The vocabulary is chosen for effect and includes some sophisticated word choices, using linguistic devices successfully. The writing is engaging and it contains a range of clear, connected ideas. A variety of sentence forms are used for effect. Grammar, punctuation and spelling (including the spelling of complex words) are all good. For example:

> Some sophisticated word choices

Old trees with white trunks grow almost everywhere. They surround the path where a woman runs. Sunlight streams between the branches. These trees are too close together to allow any foliage *to appear. A few of their rope-like roots can be seen in the grass. The trees stand quite close to the path. None of them dares to touch it.*

In the centre of this scene is the woman. She is wearing blue jeans and a black anorak with a furry hood. Her feet run rapidly uphill. Her long brown hair flies in the wind. She *seems happy. Her steps are light. In fact, it looks like she could fly at any moment.*

> It would be better to avoid starting too many sentences with 'She' and 'Her'

> Use of linguistic devices (alliteration)

Most of the trees are buckled, bent or bowed *as if they should not grow straight in this place. The trunks at the front are darker than those behind them, suggesting they might be dead. Another twig snaps. This fragility contrasts the joyful movements of the young woman who is busy hopping and skipping between them.*

> Overall comment: This answer would benefit from more variety in sentence forms

Higher Level: This answer is confidently matched to purpose and audience; vocabulary is extensive and ambitious and writing is compelling and fluently linked, using a full range of sentence forms for effect. Grammar, punctuation and spelling (including the spelling of ambitious vocabulary) are all excellent. For example:

Ambitious vocabulary

The 's' sounds here create sibilance

Use of the senses (sound)

Variety of sentence forms and range of punctuation

> *Ghostly arms reach out at contorted angles, stiff knees and knuckles shift slightly in the breeze. These trees are watching … their roots slipping slowly down banks, their claw-like feet creeping closer to the stranger. She skips along an uneven path oblivious to their enmity.*
>
> *Beneath her feet, stones fly back. They launch spasmodic attacks at the roots. The girl never sees her enemy for she is focusing on the light that flickers close to the horizon.*
>
> *The whispering sea of grass parts as she sails its channel, her black hood billowing behind her like a wind chute.*
>
> *From somewhere far away a bird calls out. It is a cuckoo taking illegal possession of another bird's nest. It is stealing their space in the same way that these trees seek to do. The road ahead rises and leans to the right. The stranger trusts it; she allows it to guide her towards a clearing that lies around the corner.*
>
> *Once she is gone, the trees will lose their power. For now they can suck up her brief burst of energy and, for a moment, relieve the agony of their ancient, aching limbs.*

Paper 2: Section A

❶ (AO1)

A   Andy Dawson claims to be devoted to his children. (T)

B   Andy Dawson dreads the end of term. (T)

C   As a writer, Andy Dawson faces fewer work complications than some other parents. (T)

D   Andy Dawson has never wanted to work in a remote location. (F)

E   Andy Dawson believes other parents share his feelings about school holidays. (T)

F   Andy Dawson is not concerned about his approaching deadline. (F)

G   The children's mother also works from home. (F)

H   Andy Dawson always gets up at 5am to work. (F)

❷ (AO1)

Possible answers

Problems associated with holidays in Text A by Andy Dawson

- It is 'impossible' to juggle work and parenting responsibilities.
- He has to get up early at 5am in order to keep to deadlines.
- The children need entertaining but he can't 'afford to' take time off work.
- The family begin to irritate each other as they get on 'each other's wick'.
- The house gets very untidy and laundry builds up into a 'domestic state of emergency'.
- He can't get on with his work due to interruptions. This makes doing work feel 'as laborious as pushing a golf ball up a custard mountain'.
- The children stay up late and 'blight' Dawson's evenings.

Problems associated with holidays in Text B by George Gissing

- People don't know how to make 'sensible use' of their days off.
- People become 'weary' in their search for the sea and cheap food.
- There is lots of 'dust' and 'dirt'.
- People are more used to working 'for work's sake' than enjoying their leisure time.
- On holiday days people 'drive wildly about the town'.
- The streets get 'overcrowded with swarms of people'.
- People get noisy, and become 'screeching drunkards'.
- The children become 'miserable' when they are 'lugged about'.

Sample student responses

Mid Level: A clear synthesis and interpretation of both texts, using relevant details and inferences and showing the differences between texts. For example:

Both writers suggest that holidays cause problems. Andy Dawson's main problem is that he has to look after his children, which means that he can't get on with his work. The children annoy him by staying up too late, asking him to play football and fix the printer. He seems to have a rather negative attitude towards his children. On the other hand, Gissing has a negative attitude towards the crowds of ordinary people who spend their bank holidays having fun outside. He claims that these people work so much that they have no idea how to enjoy a proper holiday.

Dawson's main problem is that he is always thinking about work and not about having fun with his children. He believes that trying to get on with his work is as 'laborious as pushing a golf ball up a custard mountain', which would be almost impossible. In contrast, Gissing focuses on how people behave badly on bank holidays and claims that they get loud and drunk.

Higher Level: A perceptive synthesis and interpretation of both texts. Well-chosen textual details are used effectively. Perceptive inferences are made from both texts, showing the differences between them: For example:

Both Andy Dawson and George Gissing think that holidays cause difficulties and they both discuss these problems in relation to work. Dawson shows no real inclination to enjoy the holidays with his children and the majority of his problems arise because of what he calls the 'impossible work/parenting juggle'. He is reduced to getting up at 5am to meet work deadlines because his children demand constant entertainment and attention.

Gissing, on the other hand, feels that the general public would like to enjoy bank holidays but they don't know how because they spend most of their time working 'for work's sake'. Furthermore, holiday chaos features in both texts: in the Dawson article there is internal chaos as the house is thrown into a 'domestic state of emergency' as laundry builds up, while Gissing describes external chaos consisting of overcrowded streets, parks full of 'screeching drunkards' and people driving about 'wildly'.

In both texts it is suggested that children cause problems during holidays. Dawson and his children find it impossible to co-exist peacefully and end up 'getting right on each other's wick'. Likewise, in the Gissing extract, miserable children cry after being 'lugged' around the town. Then they are 'beaten because they yell' which causes more misery.

❸ (AO2)

Possible answers

- Gissing states that the streets are 'overcrowded' and that the people 'rush in crowds'. The noun 'crowds' suggests that holidaymakers may be following others rather than doing what they want.
- The verb 'rush' implies haste which is not something associated with peace or relaxation.
- The people are described rushing to 'some sweltering place'. The adjective 'sweltering' implies somewhere unbearably hot, which would be uncomfortable.
- Gissing explains that people 'sit and drink and quarrel themselves into stupidity'. His repetition of the conjunction 'and' implies a connected sequence of events. People who are quarrelling are not happy.
- The noun 'stupidity' implies that people drink themselves senseless and this could prevent them from enjoying their holiday.
- The children are clearly unhappy as they are described using the adjective 'miserable'. We are also told that children are 'lugged' about. The verb 'to lug' means to carry with difficulty and this implies the children are viewed as a burden.
- These children are 'yelling at the top of their voices, and are beaten because they yell'. Their distress is punished by their parents who are presumably unhappy about the noise.
- Those who go to the seaside 'succeed in wearying themselves to death'. The phrase 'to death' is often used to convey negative emotions.
- The adjective 'greasy' is used to describe a 'meal in a Margate Coffee-shop'. Greasy food is oily and it would not be enjoyable to eat.
- When people try to look at the sea, they find their eyes are 'blinded with dirt and perspiration'. The nouns 'dirt' and 'perspiration' are both negative and make readers think that the people are physically uncomfortable.
- This idea of dirt is supported by another sentence employing the conjunction 'and': 'one general mass of dust and heat and rage and exhaustion'. Here the 'ands' extend the sentence to suggest that the people's suffering was long-term. This sentence also reminds us that the people were hot, quarrelling, tired and dirty.

Sample student responses

Mid Level: A clear understanding of language with relevant details, effects explained and accurate use of terminology. For example:

The writer describes the unpleasant conditions that people have to endure on bank holidays. They go to 'sweltering' places and 'rush' about in 'crowds'. This would make anybody feel unhappy as rushing about in the heat is not pleasant.

The children are described using the adjective 'miserable' and their parents smack them when they cry. They are 'lugged about, yelling at the top of their voices', which shows us that they were very unhappy. The verb 'lugged' suggests they are being dragged about, which seems like their parents don't care about their feelings much.

Gissing also uses very negative language to describe a trip to the seaside where the food is 'greasy' and the people's eyes get 'blinded with dirt and perspiration'. This would not be what they expected when they set off for a day trip and it would probably make them unhappy.

The writer also tells us that the parks and commons are full of 'screeching drunkards' and 'screeching' sounds noisy and unpleasant. There is also a long sentence describing a mass of 'dust and heat and rage and exhaustion' which sounds like nobody is happy because they are hot, grumpy and tired.

Higher Level: A detailed and perceptive understanding of language with relevant details, effects explained and sophisticated and accurate use of terminology. For example:

Throughout this extract Gissing uses language associated with heat, dirt, anger and overcrowding to suggest that holidays make people unhappy. Holiday makers are described as rushing 'in crowds' to 'sweltering' places. The adjective 'sweltering' gives us an impression of uncomfortable heat while the noun 'crowds' suggests that nobody has room to move. He develops this initial picture of suffering by using the adjective 'miserable' to describe the children who are 'lugged' about by their parents and beaten when they 'yell'. The verb 'lugged' implies that parents view their children as burdens and we could infer that they were probably smacked because their crying was an irritation to the adults.

Gissing makes a trip to the seaside sound very unappealing as he lists a number of possible causes of unhappiness. A café meal is described using the adjective 'greasy' which makes it sound oily and unappetising. The people weary themselves 'to death' and this phrase has very negative connotations. Eyes are blinded with 'dirt and perspiration', two nouns that develop the impression of heat and dirtiness.

Gissing twice uses the conjunction 'and' to extend sentences which describe people's unhappiness. Initially he states that people 'sit and drink and quarrel themselves into stupidity'. In this instance, his use of 'and' suggests a process of unfortunate but interconnected events. Quarrelling is not something that we normally associate with happiness and being drunk would also prevent any real enjoyment of the holiday. Near the end of his first paragraph, Gissing uses the word 'and' in a similar way when he describes people as 'one general mass of dust and heat and rage and exhaustion'. Here the conjunction is used to draw the reader's attention to each of the problems the holidaymakers face. This sentence also supports many of Gissing's earlier points since 'dust' reminds us of 'dirt', 'heat' reminds us of 'sweltering' and 'perspiration', 'rage' reminds us that the people are quarrelling and 'exhaustion' can be linked to the idea of people wearying themselves 'to death'.

④ (AO3)

Possible answers

- Both writers seem to have predominantly negative feelings about holidays.
- Dawson feels that there is no time for work during the holidays, which become an 'impossible work/ parenting juggle'.
- Gissing suggests there is no time for leisure in working life so people don't know how to relax when they are on holiday.
- The two men adopt very different tones.
- Dawson's tone is humorous and his feelings are conveyed in an amusing way, often through deliberate over-exaggeration such as 'breaking out in cold sweats'.
- He addresses the reader directly, using the word 'you' in order to encourage us to empathise with his feelings, and he shares amusing domestic anecdotes.
- Gissing writes from a more distant, judgemental position, remaining detached from the scenes he describes.
- Gissing feels that holidays make children 'miserable' and then their parents beat them 'because they yell'.
- Dawson feels that his children deliberately make him suffer as they have invented 'some sort of unspoken tag system' to make sure that he is constantly interrupted.
- The structure of each text reveals the writer's feelings.
- Gissing opens his letter with an immediate description of streets crowded 'with swarms of people'. The collective noun 'swarms' is usually used to describe flies or bees.
- He uses another animalistic term when he refers to holidaymakers as 'hideous creatures'.
- In his article, Dawson implies that the holidays soon have him 'clawing at (his) own skin'. The term 'clawing' is also associated with animals.
- In his second paragraph, Gissing changes to a more reflective tone as he tries to suggest that work is the cause of holiday problems.

- Dawson also becomes reflective when he thinks about 'how much of the strain of child-rearing is carried by the education system'.

Sample student responses

Mid Level: Ideas and perspectives are compared in a clear and relevant way with reference to writers' methods. A clear understanding of the different ideas and perspectives in both texts is conveyed using relevant details. For example:

Dawson reveals his feelings about holidays in a humorous way by encouraging us to imagine incidents from his own life. He involves readers directly in the action by using the word 'you' throughout his article. He feels that holidays interrupt his work, but as he has a deadline to meet, he gets very irritated by his children, although he tries not to show this as he wants to be a good father.

Gissing draws attention to the way that people behave on holidays and he seems to feel that their behaviour is totally inappropriate. He appears to judge others and to view them from a very critical viewpoint. He calls them 'hideous creatures', which suggests that he feels they are behaving like animals, and he clearly disapproves of their drunken 'screeching'.

Both writers suggest that children cause irritation during holidays. Dawson is annoyed because his children keep deliberately interrupting him, while Gissing observes children being 'lugged' about and then yelling, which makes their parents smack them.

After spending a whole paragraph expressing his critical views about holidaymakers, Gissing attempts to explain why people can't enjoy their leisure. He feels that it would be better to give them shorter working days rather than bank holidays because then they might learn how to enjoy themselves. Dawson devotes most of his article to explaining why he feels so frustrated but he does so in an amusing way by sharing a number of anecdotes to illustrate his feelings. For example, the girl interrupts him because she 'wants to know if she can have some strawberries'. I think this is funny because it seems very realistic

Higher Level: Ideas and perspectives are compared perceptively by analysing writers' methods and showing a detailed understanding of the different ideas and perspectives, using well-chosen details from both texts. For example:

Both Andy Dawson and George Gissing have negative feelings about holidays but while Dawson suggests that it is the holidays that stop him being able to work, because of the 'impossible work/parenting juggle', Gissing implies that it is work that stops people enjoying their holidays since most of them 'work for work's sake' and don't know how to relax.

Dawson adopts a humorous, conversational, tone. He shares amusing anecdotes from his life and addresses the reader as 'you' to encourage empathy. Gissing writes from a more detached position which could infer that he feels superior to most holidaymakers because he dislikes crowded noisy places and prefers 'the pleasure of peace and quietness'. His use of alliteration emphasises the value of such tranquillity. Dawson also dreams of relaxing during summer evenings but he feels that holidays 'blight' this precious free time because of 'extensions to regular bedtimes'. The word 'blight' implies that his free time is spoilt and disrupted.

Disruption is indeed a key theme for both writers. Gissing criticises those who disturb the peace by driving 'wildly about the town in gigs, donkey-carts, cabbage-carts, dirt-carts'. It is noticeable that these carts all have negative implications, as if they are unsuitable for people. His reference to 'dirt-carts' also supports his ongoing suggestion that holidays cause mess, filth and 'dust'. Similarly, Dawson acknowledges that holidays can become chaotic when he loses control of the chores and the living room resembles 'a toy shop that has been ransacked in a riot'.

Both writers use derogatory language to reveal their feelings about others. Gissing refers to drunken holidaymakers 'screeching', a sound normally associated with birds, while Dawson claims that his children are 'mooching' about, implying that they may be bored or listless. He is clearly irritated when he suggests that his children have developed 'some

sort of innate, unspoken tag team system' in order to make sure that he is constantly pestered. Gissing also implies that children annoy their parents since they beat them 'because they yell'.

The benefits of holiday outings and excursions are discussed in both texts but here the writers' feelings clearly differ. Dawson feels that there are 'majestic' places to visit, but Gissing paints a grim picture of a visit to the seaside where visitors can only glimpse the sea through 'eyes blinded with dirt and perspiration'.

The structure of these texts is designed to reveal more about the writers' feelings. Gissing begins his piece with an immediate description of bank holiday chaos where 'streets are overcrowded with swarms of people'. Interestingly, we would normally use the collective noun 'swarms' to describe flies or wasps. He is implying that holidays dehumanise people, and this can also be seen when he calls the holidaymakers 'hideous creatures'. Similarly, Dawson feels that holidays cause negative transformations. He suggests that school holidays reduce him to a point where he is 'clawing at (his) own skin'. This description is clearly an example of humorous exaggeration but, like 'swarms', 'clawing' is a term normally associated with animals.

Once Gissing has given vent to his critical feelings, he becomes more reflective in the second half of his letter. He tries to explain why holidays are so problematic by suggesting that people spend too much time working. Dawson also becomes reflective when he realises 'how much of the strain of child-rearing is carried by the education system'.

Turn over for Question 5 answers

Paper 2: Section B

 (AO5) (AO6)

Sample student responses

Lower Level: Sometimes matched to purpose and audience. There is an attempt to use a varied vocabulary and some linguistic devices. At times the writing is clear and contains linked, relevant ideas with occasional variety in sentence structures. Some of the grammar and spelling is correct. For example:

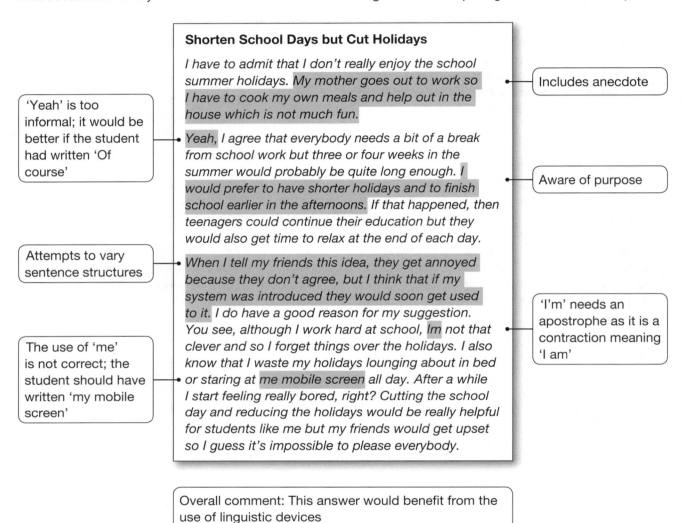

Shorten School Days but Cut Holidays

I have to admit that I don't really enjoy the school summer holidays. My mother goes out to work so I have to cook my own meals and help out in the house which is not much fun.

Yeah, I agree that everybody needs a bit of a break from school work but three or four weeks in the summer would probably be quite long enough. I would prefer to have shorter holidays and to finish school earlier in the afternoons. If that happened, then teenagers could continue their education but they would also get time to relax at the end of each day.

When I tell my friends this idea, they get annoyed because they don't agree, but I think that if my system was introduced they would soon get used to it. I do have a good reason for my suggestion. You see, although I work hard at school, Im not that clever and so I forget things over the holidays. I also know that I waste my holidays lounging about in bed or staring at me mobile screen all day. After a while I start feeling really bored, right? Cutting the school day and reducing the holidays would be really helpful for students like me but my friends would get upset so I guess it's impossible to please everybody.

Annotations:
- Includes anecdote
- Aware of purpose
- 'I'm' needs an apostrophe as it is a contraction meaning 'I am'
- 'Yeah' is too informal; it would be better if the student had written 'Of course'
- Attempts to vary sentence structures
- The use of 'me' is not correct; the student should have written 'my mobile screen'

Overall comment: This answer would benefit from the use of linguistic devices

Mid Level: Generally well matched to purpose and audience. The vocabulary is chosen for effect and includes some sophisticated word choices, using linguistic devices successfully. The writing is engaging and it contains a range of clear, connected ideas. A variety of sentence forms are used for effect. Grammar, punctuation and spelling (including the spelling of complex words) are all good. For example:

Leave My Summer Holidays Alone!

All through the school year, teenagers like me work hard for weeks on end. It's a dull routine consisting of the same boring lessons but I willingly put up with it. Why, because I've always got the long summer break to look forward to. However, some interfering adults have started suggesting that the summer holidays are too long. Instead of enjoying the summer months relaxing, they want me to spend even longer slogging away at school because English, Maths and Science are vital for my future. Yes, I know these subjects are important but I might enjoy them more if I am given a break from them sometimes!!

Who says that the summer holidays make kids bored? I'm never bored for a moment! Perhaps a few nerds get restless in the summer but I happen to think that holidays are an important part of my education. When I meet my mates in town for coffee or a shopping trip we chat all the time and that must be helping to improve my social skills. I don't get much opportunity to practise like that in school. If I start talking to friends in a lesson, I bet some grumpy teacher will soon put an end to our discussions.

It has also been claimed that taking a break will make teenagers forget everything they know. That is ridiculous! If it was true then nobody would learn anything and a baby would always say 'mama and dada'. People are designed to remember things and I think that the school curriculum is drummed into teenagers well enough to make it stick.

In my view, school holidays are really important. I'd hate to have to work day and night just because some expert decides that shorter holidays are his latest, greatest idea. On the other hand, I do understand the value of getting a good education. If teenagers are allowed to keep a balance between work and holiday time, then everyone should stay happy. So please leave our summer holidays alone!

Annotations:

- Use of connective
- Uses a rhetorical question
- Uses a short emphatic sentence to express strong feelings; uses punctuation for effect
- Unnecessary to use two exclamation marks
- Informal/colloquial: it would be better to say 'friends'
- This answer is well matched to purpose

Overall comment: This student could use more sophisticated vocabulary

Higher Level: This answer is confidently matched to purpose and audience; vocabulary is extensive and ambitious and writing is compelling and fluently linked, using a full range of sentence forms for effect. Grammar, punctuation and spelling (including the spelling of ambitious vocabulary) are all excellent. For example:

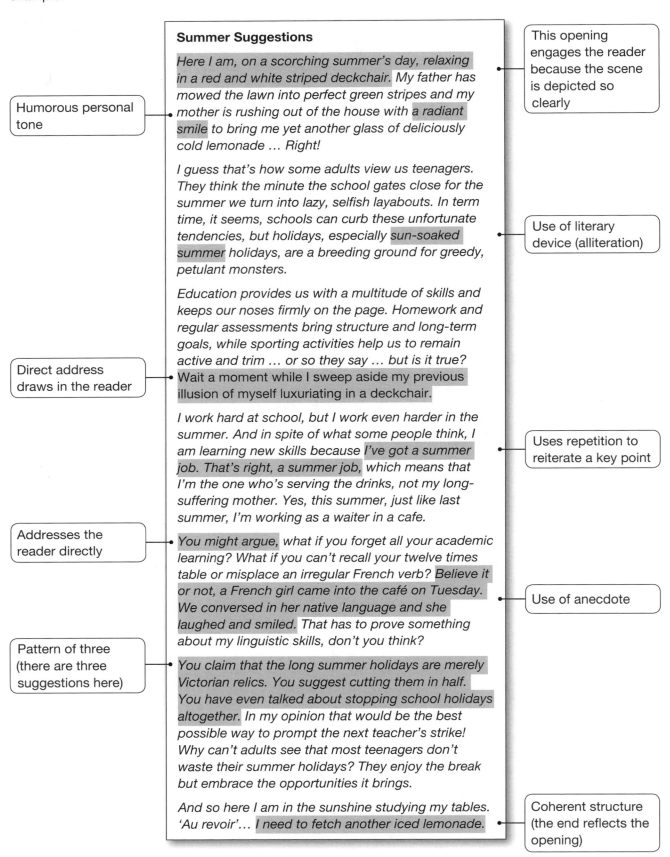

Summer Suggestions

Here I am, on a scorching summer's day, relaxing in a red and white striped deckchair. My father has mowed the lawn into perfect green stripes and my mother is rushing out of the house with a radiant smile to bring me yet another glass of deliciously cold lemonade … Right!

I guess that's how some adults view us teenagers. They think the minute the school gates close for the summer we turn into lazy, selfish layabouts. In term time, it seems, schools can curb these unfortunate tendencies, but holidays, especially sun-soaked summer holidays, are a breeding ground for greedy, petulant monsters.

Education provides us with a multitude of skills and keeps our noses firmly on the page. Homework and regular assessments bring structure and long-term goals, while sporting activities help us to remain active and trim … or so they say … but is it true? Wait a moment while I sweep aside my previous illusion of myself luxuriating in a deckchair.

I work hard at school, but I work even harder in the summer. And in spite of what some people think, I am learning new skills because I've got a summer job. That's right, a summer job, which means that I'm the one who's serving the drinks, not my long-suffering mother. Yes, this summer, just like last summer, I'm working as a waiter in a cafe.

You might argue, what if you forget all your academic learning? What if you can't recall your twelve times table or misplace an irregular French verb? Believe it or not, a French girl came into the café on Tuesday. We conversed in her native language and she laughed and smiled. That has to prove something about my linguistic skills, don't you think?

You claim that the long summer holidays are merely Victorian relics. You suggest cutting them in half. You have even talked about stopping school holidays altogether. In my opinion that would be the best possible way to prompt the next teacher's strike! Why can't adults see that most teenagers don't waste their summer holidays? They enjoy the break but embrace the opportunities it brings.

And so here I am in the sunshine studying my tables. 'Au revoir'… I need to fetch another iced lemonade.

Humorous personal tone

This opening engages the reader because the scene is depicted so clearly

Use of literary device (alliteration)

Direct address draws in the reader

Uses repetition to reiterate a key point

Addresses the reader directly

Use of anecdote

Pattern of three (there are three suggestions here)

Coherent structure (the end reflects the opening)